Information Problem-Solving:
The Big Six Skills© Approach to
Library & Information Skills Instruction

INFORMATION MANAGEMENT, POLICY, AND SERVICES
Charles R. McClure and Peter Hernon, Editors

Information Problem-Solving:
The Big Six Skills© Approach to
Library & Information Skills Instruction

Michael B. Eisenberg

Syracuse University
Syracuse, New York

Robert E. Berkowitz
Wayne Central School District
Ontario Center, New York

ABLEX PUBLISHING CORPORATION
NORWOOD, NEW JERSEY

Fourth Printing 1996

Library of Congress Cataloging-in-Publication Data

Eisenberg, Michael B.
    Information problem-solving : the big six skills approach to
library & information skills instruction / by Michael B. Eisenberg,
Robert E. Berkowitz.
        p.   cm. -- (Information management, policy, and services)
    Includes bibliographical references and index.
    ISBN 0-89391-757-5
    1. Library orientation.   2. School children--Library orientation.
3. Information retrieval--Study and teaching.   4. Information
services--User education.   5. Problem solving--Study and teaching.
I. Berkowitz, Robert E.   II. Title.   III. Series.
Z711.2.E45   1990   90-22681
                                                               CIP

Ablex Publishing Corporation
355 Chestnut St.
Norwood, NJ 07648

Contents

Figures

To our parents,

Lenny and Lenore Eisenberg

Anne and Sid Berkowitz

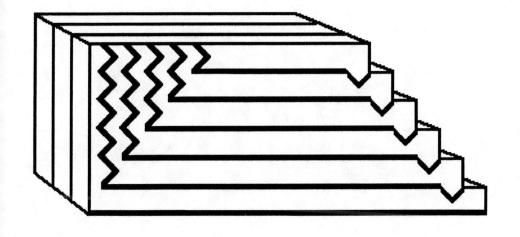

Acknowledgments

This is our second major collaboration. While we benefit from our differing perspectives, we are keenly aware of the contributions of others. From across the country, our school library media specialist professional colleagues submitted exemplary integrated library & information skills units for consideration. The variety and excellence of these submissions are indications of the growing strength of library & information skills instructional programs. Likewise, our graduate students, particularly those who were in the Summer 1989 Curriculum Concerns for Media Specialists course at Syracuse University (IST 762), promoted discussions that directly influenced the content and direction of this book. We also wish to recognize Dr. Donald P. Ely for his boundless encouragement and intellectual energy. We rely on the exchange of ideas among colleagues – current and future professionals – to push us to refine our philosophy, concepts, and methods.

Equally vital to the effort of producing a book are those who unselfishly contribute energy, enthusiasm, and expertise. We are grateful for the support of the entire School of Information Studies *crew*, in particular, to Beth Mahoney and Natalie Blando for turning a rough manuscript into a camera-ready book; to Linda Schamber for another editing job well done; and to Chuck McClure for the opportunity to publish. A special thank you goes to Kathy Spitzer, a multi-talented individual, whose assistance is evident throughout this book.

All of our efforts are made richer by our families. Through our children, Brian and Laura Eisenberg, Adam and Marette Berkowitz, we are able to experience firsthand the joys and frustrations of getting an education in the information age. Brian helped with graphics and production for this book and for *Curriculum Initiative*, and each of the others made key contributions to both books. And most importantly, we thank our wives, Carol Eisenberg and Joyce Berkowitz, for their unique perspectives, encouragement, and of course, patience.

Mike Eisenberg & Bob Berkowitz
June 1990

About the Authors

Michael B. Eisenberg (PhD Syracuse University, MLS State University of New York at Albany), is an Associate Professor at the School of Information Studies, Syracuse University. His research and teaching interests include management and curriculum concerns of school media programs, the use of information systems by end users, and the measurement and evaluation of information systems. In addition to teaching and research, Mike is the Director at the ERIC Clearinghouse on Information Resources. His 1986 doctoral thesis, *Magnitude Estimation and the Measurement of Relevance*, won national awards from both the American Society for Information Science and the Association for Library and Information Science Education. Mike is chair of the AASL Research Committee, member of the Editorial Board of *School Library Media Quarterly*, and editor of the Current Research Column. Mike's publications include: guest editor for the special issue on technology, *School Library Media Quarterly* (Spring 1990), "Order Effects: A Study of the Possible Influence of Presentation Order on User Judgments of Document Relevance," (with C. Barry) *Journal of the American Society for Information Science* (September 1988), "Measuring Relevance Judgments," *Information Processing and Management* (1988), "Curriculum Mapping and Implementation of an Elementary School Library Media Skills Program," *School Library Media Quarterly* (Fall 1984), "Managing the Library and Information Skills Program," *School Library Media Activities Monthly* (March 1986). Mike is a frequent speaker at conferences, and presents a number of workshops and training sessions each year. He has worked as a teacher, school library media specialist, program administrator, and consultant.

Robert E. Berkowitz, (MA in Education George Washington University, MLS State University of New York at Albany, School Administrator's Certification, North Adams (Massachusetts) State College) is a School Library Media Specialist with the Wayne Central School District, Ontario Center, NY. Bob has successfully managed school libraries grades Head Start - 12 in both rural and urban settings. He has been an educational professional since 1971. Bob is a strong believer in goals-oriented management, the library media specialist as a key partner in the excellence in education - effective schools movement, and the integration of critical thinking skills into library & information skills instruction. Putting these ideas into action, Bob acted as Library Media Specialist Consultant to a research skills-based English curriculum project that won National Council of Teachers of English recognition as a Center of Excellence in English and the Language Arts.

Bob is an Adjunct Instructor at Syracuse University's School of Information Studies, and Visiting Lecturer at State University of New York at Buffalo's School of Information and Library Studies. He is often requested to share his ideas at conferences and seminars. Bob is the author of: "Thinking is Critical: Moving Students Beyond Location," *School Library Media Activities Monthly* (May 1987), "When Information Skills Meet Science Curriculum: a cooperative effort," *School Library Media Activities Monthly* (June 1988), and "School Libraries: Emerging Centers for Life-Long Learning," *The Bookmark* (Winter 1989). Bob has a strong commitment to library media specialists shaping their own professional future.

Mike and Bob have collaborated on a number of books and projects, most notably *Curriculum Initiative: An Agenda and Strategy for Library Media Programs* (Ablex Publishing Corp., 1988), and *Resource Companion to Curriculum Initiative* (Ablex Publishing Corp., 1988).

Foreword:

What follows is a script for a docu-drama, in fact two scripts displayed side by side. In each situation, a library media specialist is teaching library skills to a group of students. In each case, the library media specialist has expectations for what students will learn. And, in each case students are responding. However, the two different instructional sequences portray distinctly different approaches. One script is an example of a library & information skills instructional lesson based on the Big Six Skills information problem-solving model. The instruction can be characterized as active, interesting, and based on a real curriculum need. The second script exemplifies a resource-based approach to library skills instruction. It is passive, uninteresting, and not tied to any curriculum context. As you read, consider which approach is more likely to meet the information needs of students, now and in the future. What would you want to have happen in your school library media center? What can you do to make that happen?

Characters:
  School Library Media Specialist
  A large class-group of students
Scene:
  School library media center,
  anywhere in the world.

[*Enter Students. School Library Media Specialist welcomes students as they come through the door. The bell rings to begin the period.*]

Library Media Specialist: Good morning! I'm glad you're all here! I understand that in social studies yesterday you were discussing culture and community. Your teacher, Mr. Donnelly, told you that one of the major group activities in our society, a reflection of our culture, is going to the movies. Mr. Donnelly also told me that as an assignment for the weekend, each of you is supposed to go to a movie with a friend

---

Characters:
  School Library Media Specialist
  A large class-group of students
Scene:
  School library media center,
  anywhere in the world.

[*Enter Students. School Library Media Specialist welcomes students as they come through the door. The Library Media Specialist is holding a copy of* Readers' Guide to Periodical Literature *in her hand. The bell rings to begin the period.*]

Library Media Specialist: Good morning! I'm glad you're all here! How many people recognize this book from last year? [*The Library Media Specialist waves the copy of* Readers' Guide to Periodical Literature *at the students.*]

Students: [*Some students groan, some hands raise, all students look bored.*]

and observe people. That sounds like a fun assignment.

Students: Yeah, Mr. Donnelly sure knows how to make sociology interesting.

Library Media Specialist: Yes, you're right, he does give interesting homework assignments. And that's why he and I decided that you should come to the library media center today, to review the assignment from an information perspective so that you can complete it successfully and have some fun at the same time. So, my job this morning is to tie this assignment to the work we've previously done together on information problem-solving. I'm sure you remember the Big Six Skills, and this chart we refer to when we talk about the Big Six. [*Library Media Specialist shows students her Big Six Skills poster.*] And, I know that you remember that we use the Big Six whenever we have library type information problems which need to be solved. Well, today I'm going to work with you a little bit to show you how the Big Six is applicable to any information problem you need to solve. As you know, we live in an information rich society. One of the keys to success in an information oriented society is the ability to solve information problems and make decisions based on information. That's what we're going to be sharpening up on today – your ability to solve information problems. [*Library Media Specialist points to the large Big Six Skills poster.*]

You remember the Big Six:
Task definition – defining what you need – from an information point of view.

Library Media Specialist:
Yes, that's right, it's the *Readers' Guide to Periodical Literature*. How many people remember how to use it?

Students: [*A few students raise their hands.*]

[*The Library Media Specialist proceeds with her lesson oblivious to student lack of interest. Students begin to exhibit inappropriate classroom behaviors.*]

Library Media Specialist: I know we did some work with the *Readers' Guide* at the beginning of last year during the orientation program, but it's important to review some of the key points about how to use it, and then I'll pass out a worksheet with some questions that you can answer using the *Readers' Guide*. As you know, the *Readers' Guide* has two points of access. Can anybody name them? [*After waiting a couple of seconds, and realizing that none of the students is going to raise a hand...*] subject and author. Both subjects and authors are listed together, in alphabetical order. Any questions?

Students: [*No students raise their hands They look and act disinterested.*]

Library Media Specialist: Good. Now, you may also come across *see* and *see also* citations. You will need to know what they mean. Also, if you have any problems using the *Readers' Guide*, there is a sample citation explained in the front of the book, and a list of the abbreviations used within the citations. If you have any questions as you do this worksheet, please refer to the front of the *Readers' Guide*. Any questions?

Information seeking strategies - where are all the possible places that you can check for information to help meet the task.

Location and access - getting to the information sources and then getting to the information in the sources.

Information use - once you get to the source, this step is using the source and getting the information that you need from the source.

Synthesis - combining all the different pieces of information into a form that meets the requirements of the original task.

Evaluation - determining the effectiveness and efficiency of your information problem-solving tactic - whether or not you successfully completed the task and if you did so in a reasonable amount of time.

Any questions about the definitions of each of the Big Six?
[*Library Media Specialist waits patiently. Receiving no response, she continues.*] OK, let's check... I'll give you the first two and last two... think about the middle two: task definition, information seeking strategies, synthesis and evaluation... Think about the other two... Write them down and I'll walk around quickly and check... While I'm doing that, write down which of the Big Six checks for effectiveness and efficiency, and which of the Big Six is concerned with developing a list of possible sources which can be used to solve an information problem. [*The Library Media Specialist walks around*

[*The Library Media Specialist begins to hand out the* Readers' Guide *worksheets.*]

[*Students speak in an argumentative, challenging tone.*]
Student: Do we have to do this?

Student: This stuff is boring!

Student: Didn't we do this worksheet last year?

Student: Why do we need to do this again?

Library Media Specialist: It's an important library resource, and I'm sorry you think it's boring, but it is important to know how to use the *Readers' Guide* if you plan to go to college someday. Any other questions? [*Students do not respond.*] Good. Here are the sheets. Please work on your own. I don't want this to be a group effort. You have the rest of the class time to finish this assignment.

[*Students begin doing the worksheet.*]
·
·
·
·
·
·

[*Library Media Specialist monitors students.*]
·
·
·
·

*the group and checks students' under-
standing of the Big Six Skills definitions.*] Everybody seems to be right on
track. Now, the question is, how does
this process, which we've labeled the
Big Six, relate to your weekend assignment? Let's consider ways to apply the
Big Six Skills approach to your problem. Once again, the overall problem –
listen carefully, and correct me if I'm
wrong – is that you and a friend or class-
mate have to go to a movie on Friday
evening and observe people using the
checksheet that Mr. Donnelly gave you.

Students: [*Show agreement.*]

Library Media Spcialist: We know
that the first step of the Big Six is Task
Definition. What needs to be done from
an information perspective? What do
you have to do – from an information
perspective? Before you answer, think
about it.

[*Students eagerly raise hands to answer
and are called on by the Library Media
Specialist. Others are motivated to blurt
out answers.*]

Student: [*Tentatively.*] We need to
find information about what's playing.

Student: Where's it playing?

Student: What time is it playing?

Student: What does my partner want to
see?

Student: How am I going to get there?

Student: Can I go to the bathroom?

Library Media Specialist: No, start
your work.

[*Students continue working on the
assignment.*]

[*Library Media Specialist monitors
students.*]

[*After a few minutes...*]
Student: But I really have to go.

Library Media Specialist: OK, but
don't take too long. You have a lot of
work to get done.

Library Media Specialist: Right! Excellent, and there are certainly other important questions you could have mentioned, and all of them are part of Task Definition. Actually, these are a series of small information problems which need to be solved. Now, what are some of the options that you have in terms of ways to meet these information needs? In other words, what Information Seeking Strategies are possible?

[*Once again, students eagerly raise hands to answer and are called on by the Library Media Specialist. Others are motivated to blurt out answers.*]

Student: The local newspaper.

Student: Ask friends.

Student: Use a phone book and call the movie houses.

Student: Drive up and down Main Street.

Student: Listen to the radio and hope there's an advertisement.

[*Library Media Specialist shows pleasure in the responses given by students.*]

Library Media Specialist: Sure, all of these are potential sources of information you might want to use to help you solve this problem. Remember, after you make your list, what do you do?

[*As a chorus .*]
Students: You go back to your original task and see if you're still on target.

[*Students continue doing their work.*]

.
.
.
.
.
.
.
.

[*Library Media Specialist monitors students.*]

.
.
.
.
.
.
.
.
.

[*The student returns. Another student speaks.*]
Student: Do we have to answer all of these? Can we just do the even numbers?

Library Media Specialist: No, you have to do all of the questions on the worksheet. Let's settle in and get some work done.

[*Students continue doing the worksheet.*]

.
.
.
.
.
.
.

Library Media Specialist: Right, and in this case we're OK. But one more thing, if you consider this list just for a minute, and you try to categorize your answers, what you'll find is that you've identified a number of sources in two basic types - text and human. There are some considerations with the Information Seeking Strategies step that we will discuss at a later time - like, what makes one source better than another: accuracy, reliability, ease of use, availability, comprehensibility, and so forth. But for now, we've identified the tasks and possible Information Seeking Strategies to follow. [*The Library Media Specialist changes the pace of the discussion once again with some rapid fire questions.*] Now, going on to do Location and Access, and Information Use together, the question you need to ask is, "where do I get the things I'm going to use to find the information?" And, "How do I use them?"

Student: Newspapers.

Library Media Specialist: Which paper? Which section of the paper? Which day? Where do you get the newspaper?

Student: At home or in the library.

Library Media Specialist: In the library? Yeah! I knew I was here for some reason! OK, where is the information about movies in the newspaper? How do you get to it?

Student: You can always use the table of contents.

Library Media Specialist: Where else? Which section of the newspaper?

.
.
.
.

[*Library Media Specialist monitors students.*]

.
.
.
.
.
.
.
.
.
.
.
.
.
.
.

Student: When's the bell gonna ring?

.
.
.
.
.
.
.
.
.
.

[*A few minutes later.*]
Student: This is dumb.

[*Students start to get restless.*]
Student: This is too hard. I'm not doing this. Did anyone go to the concert last night?

Student: The entertainment section. You can read all the ads.

Library Media Specialist: Exactly. What are some other places to find information about movies?

[*Chorus.*]
Students: Use a phone book, and call up movie houses.

Library Media Specialist: OK, where do you get the phone book?

Student: At home, in the library.

Library Media Specialist: And how would you find the numbers?

Student: Use the yellow pages, look under movies.

Library Media Specialist: Maybe. Remember that reference books like the phone book can list information in places you might not expect... you may have to check under some other headings like theaters or films. Let's say that you found the list of phone numbers for the movie theaters, and you call. What are you likely to get?

Student: A recording.

Library Media Specialist: Right, a recording. So, when should you call?

[*Chorus.*]
Students: When the box office is open.

Library Media Specialist: That's a good idea. Let's think of other alternatives... like... what about driving up and down the strip? You could just drive

Library Media Specialist: Get back to work, please.

Student: No, my Mom wouldn't let me go.

Student: Awesome, an awesome concert... you should have been there... [*louder*] All of you should have been there!

[*Students lose focus and start talking.*]

[*Interrupting in a loud voice.*]

Library Media Specialist: That's quite enough. Your job is to get this work done!

Student: I'm not doing anything!

Student: Yeah, he wasn't.

[*Students continue to work.*]

.
.
.
.
.
.
.
.
.

.

[*Library Media Specialist monitors students.*]

.
.
.
.
.

along past the movie theaters until you find something you think you'll like.

Student: Asking friends is another alternative.

Library Media Specialist: How do you locate and access information from a friend?

Student: Find him in school and ask him if he's seen any good movies lately.

Student: Call her at home after school.

Student: You may have to use the phone book, or the information operator to get her number.

Library Media Specialist: Using this kind of information source, a human source, happens through a personal conversation or a note. [*The Library Media Specialist changes the pace of the instruction once again.*] Now onto the fifth, second to last step in the Big Six. Synthesis. Synthesis means bringing it all together to solve the information problem. In successfully meeting the requirement of this weekend's assignment, you need to bring together the information about the movies with some other aspects of the *event* such as date, food, and maybe other related activities – all of which can be seen as a series of interrelated information problems to be solved. So, what have you got so far that needs to be coordinated?

Student: A few movie choices.

Student: Times.

Student: Dates.

Student: Can I go to the boys' room?

[*Losing patience.*]
Library Media Specialist: I said, that's enough. Get back to work, now!

[*Students go back to working on their assignment.*]

Student: Stuff the other guys want to do.

Student: Mom's car.

Library Media Specialist: Right. And there are probably many more variables if we took some more time to list them. So, the task now is to bring it all together – organize the information and compare information aspects one to another. How might you do that?

Student: Make a list.

Student: Talk it over with a friend.

Student: Make a chart.

Student: Write a note.

Student: Do it in my head.

Library Media Specialist: OK, fine, fine, these are all ways to organize information. Now, how do we make the information available to those people who need it? First, who needs this information?

[Students are still attentive and eagerly raise hands to answer. They are called on by the Library Media Specialist. Others are motivated to blurt out answers.]

Students: Friends.

Student: Classmates.

Student: Other students.

Student: The teacher.

Student: My parents.

[Library Media Specialist monitors students.]

.
.
.
.
.
.
.
.
.
.
.
.
.
.

[After quite a few minutes.]
Student: How come we're doing this anyway?

Library Media Specialist: Quiet!
[The Library Media Specialist struggles to keep the class quiet ... and then...]
Who hasn't finished yet?

[Some students raise their hands. Some students look over at the clock.]

Student: I'm finished.

Student: I'm not finished yet.

Student: Me too, I'm just on number 7.

Student: Yeah, I got a lot more to do.

Library Media Specialist: OK, a few more minutes and then we'll go over the answers.

Library Media Specialist: How can you present the choices or alternatives to them?

Student: Talk to the class as a group.

Student: Post a note on the bulletin board.

Student: Telephone calls.

Student: Write a note to the teacher.

[*Library Media Specialist shows pleasure in the responses given by students.*]

Library Media Specialist: Great. And these are just some of the ways to present information. And, these are all ways to communicate synthesized information. Now, do they need to be given all the information you find? Maybe, but just as likely not. They just need the facts, which are:

[*Chorus.*]
Students: Movie, time, place.

Library Media Specialist: Sure!... and that's *adding value* to information - when you sift through the unimportant information and give only the essential, important information, that's adding value. [*The Library Media Specialist changes the pace of the instruction once again.*] Finally, the last step... evaluation. As you know from solving other information problems, it is important to evaluate how well you do from two perspectives. First, ask yourself "Was I successful in achieving the task?" that's effectiveness. And second, ask yourself, "Was the process I used easy and did it take a reasonable amount of time

[*Students continue with the worksheet.*]

[*Library Media Specialist monitors students.*]

to finish?" that's efficiency. I've said it before, and I'll say it again, a good information problem-solver is both effective and efficient. I know that we've talked about a number of important ideas and strategies this morning. I'm sure you will agree with me that it's important to have a strategy when you need to answer any kind of information problem. And, if you have a strategy which you can use all the time, one that works well for you, there are lots of uses - such as when you have to make a decision based on a set of information, interpret a graph or chart, etc. If there are no questions at this point, I think you ought to begin planning how you're going to get to that movie this weekend.

[*Students spend the remainder of the class time planning. The bell to end the class period rings. The Library Media Specialist dismisses her students.*]

Library Media Specialist: Have a great day everybody. Enjoy the movie.

[*Students leave the library. The Library Media Specialist is pleased with her students' performance.*]

[*After a few more minutes in which some students are working and others are talking or fooling around...*]

Library Media Specialist: Well, all right... let's go over the answers. Who has the answer for question number one? [*The Library Media Specialist waits...*] Number one?

[*The bell rings for students to move on to the next class. Before the Library Media Specialist can respond, students stand up and get ready to leave the room. Some students start to move toward the door. Some sudents leave their papers on the tables, others stuff them into folders or packs. Sudents begin to walk out of the library.*]

Library Media Specialist: Everyone take your papers. We'll go over them tomorrow.

[*The rest of the students leave the library. The Library Media Specialist goes around and picks up the papers left by the students as the next class walks into the Library Media Center for their lesson.*]

This book champions the Big Six Skills approach to library & information skills instruction. It is an approach based on information problem-solving, taught through integration with subject area curriculum, and generalizable to all information problem situations. The Big Six Skills approach gives students the competence and confidence necessary to meet a lifetime of information needs. A library & information skills instructional program of this kind is essential to education in a changing world.

Introduction

The concept of a general problem-solving approach to library & information skills instruction was presented in our previous book, *Curriculum Initiative: An Agenda and Strategy for Library Media Programs* (Ablex 1988). We labeled this approach the *Big Six Skills** in order to emphasize the importance of each of six skill areas in the problem-solving process.

The positive response to the Big Six Skills approach has been overwhelming. Library media specialists, teachers, and administrators quickly grasp the power and simplicity of teaching information problem-solving as a generalizable process. More than one library media specialist has commented that the name "Big Six Skills" understates the significance of this highly conceptual model that takes traditional library skills instruction to a new level.

Actually, the phrase *The Big Six Skills* has taken on at least three meanings. The Big Six Skills represents:

(1) a systematic approach to information problem-solving. It is appropriate and useful to initiate the six logical steps** *whenever an individual has an information-oriented problem.*

(2) six broad skill areas necessary for successful information problem-solving. Students need to develop a range of competencies within each skill area.

(3) a complete library & information skills curriculum. Often referred to as a *scope and sequence*, the Big Six Skills offers a systematic alternative to traditional K-12 frameworks that focus on location and access skills.

Curriculum Initiative: An Agenda and Strategy for Library Media Programs is more than the Big Six Skills. It is a book tightly packed with ideas and approaches. As the subtitle states, it lays out a curriculum-based agenda for library media programs, and specific strategies for implementing that agenda. The Big Six Skills is just one part of that agenda.

---

*   The phrases "Big Six," "Big Six Skills," and "Big Six Skills Curriculum" are all registered copyrights of the authors. Permission is granted for full use of these terms provided that recognition is properly and duly noted.

**   Although described as six logical steps, the Big Six Skills process is not necessarily sequential. In solving information problems, a person often loops back to a prior step. This is explained in more detail in Chapter 1.

Almost immediately upon publication of *Curriculum Initiative*, it became clear that we would need to further articulate the Big Six Skills in another publication. *Curriculum Initiative* offered some examples, but did not fully develop the approach or provide detailed assistance to library media professionals and teachers interested in implementing a Big Six Skills approach. Also, *Curriculum Initiative* stressed the critical thinking aspects of the Big Six Skills. The Big Six Skills is definitely based in critical thinking. However, in working with groups, individuals, and classes, we found that the most effective ways to help educators grasp the Big Six Skills approach are to stress the overall information problem-solving perspective and to offer clear definitions and examples of each of the Big Six Skills.

Therefore, this book goes beyond *Curriculum Initiative* by:

- presenting the Big Six Skills from multiple perspectives

- providing exercises, examples, and explanations to help the reader fully understand the specifics of the Big Six Skills

- suggesting practical methods for bringing together existing instructional efforts and the Big Six Skills information problem-solving approach

- giving specific examples of Big Six Skills instruction that is integrated with content curriculum units.

The book begins with definitions and explanations of the Big Six Skills approach, moves to a discussion of implementation, and concludes with specific exemplary instructional units and lessons.

- Chapter 1 revisits the overarching concepts and themes of the approach.

- Chapter 2 defines and explains an expanded view of the increasingly specific levels of the Big Six Skills.

- Chapter 3 provides contextual examples and exercises to develop a better understanding of the Big Six Skills.

- Chapter 4 focuses on practical actions that relate to planning and implementation of the Big Six Skills approach.

- Chapter 5 offers exemplary integrated instructional units to act as models for elementary and secondary settings.

- Chapter 6 provides examples of generic lessons that can be easily adapted to assist in delivering the desired integrated instruction.

Together, these chapters emphasize practical and tested techniques to develop and implement library & information skills instructional programs based on the Big Six Skills approach.

Chapter 1
The Big Six Skills Revisited

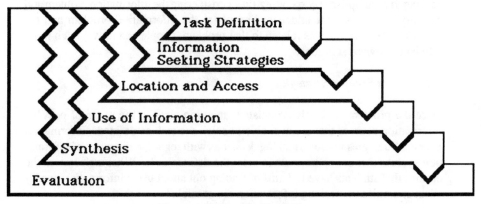

Figure 1.1: The Big Six Skills

**THE BIG SIX SKILLS APPROACH TO
INFORMATION PROBLEM-SOLVING**

As noted in the introduction, the Big Six Skills perspective represents a general approach to information problem-solving consisting of six logical steps or stages (see figure 1.1). Each stage is necessary for the successful resolution of an information problem. However, the exact order of stages and the amount of time spent on a given stage may vary greatly from situation to situation. Each skill area is briefly outlined below. An expanded explanation of the overall model as well as specific examples are offered in Chapter 2.

Task Definition

Information problem-solving begins with a clear understanding of the problem at hand *from an information point of view.* In order to solve an information problem, students need to determine the range and nature of tasks to be accomplished. For more general problems, students need to determine the information aspects of the problem: what are the questions that need to be answered, what kind of information do they need in order to tackle the problem.

When students are involved in the process of recognizing that they have an information problem to solve or a decision to make that is dependent on informa-

5

tion, they are involved in task definition. Task definition includes stating the parameters of the problem from an information needs perspective.

Most people spend too little time on task definition. The tendency is to push ahead even though they have only a general or vague understanding of what it is they are seeking to accomplish. By spending time considering the information problem and then articulating a clear understanding of (a) the information problem and (b) specific information needs related to that problem, people can move much more efficiently toward solutions.

Information Seeking Strategies

Once the problem is clearly articulated, attention turns to the range of possible information sources that are available to solve the task as defined. Information Seeking Strategies involves making decisions with regard to the range of information sources that are appropriate to meet the defined task. What are some of the options that students have in terms of finding out about these information needs? What strategies for seeking information are possible?

We live in an information-rich world. According to *Megatrends* (Naisbitt, 1982), over 6,000 scientific articles are written *each day*, and science and technological information *doubles* every 5.5 years! Large (1984) states that "more new information [has been produced] in thirty years than in the previous 5,000. About a thousand new book titles are published each day throughout the world and the total of all printed knowledge is doubling every eight years." (p. 46) This *explosion of information* has serious implications for information seeking by all persons, but especially for students.

For example, in most cases there is not just one *right* source of information to answer an information need; there are likely to be a number of alternative sources and approaches that can successfully lead to resolution of the problem. The question becomes less, "Can I find information on this topic?" and more "What are my *best* strategies for finding information on this topic?"

The world of information can be broken down into two fundamental categories: text and human. Text encompasses the full range of printed and computer-based information resources, and includes nonbook media as well (e.g., audio recordings, video recordings, graphics). All the materials in libraries and media centers can be classified as text. The human category refers to information gained from another person, through some form of direct contact (in-person, via telephone or some other form of telecommunications). Broadcast radio and television can be considered in the human category.

When students consider Information Seeking Strategies, they should be encouraged to include the full range of potential sources in both categories. Choices are narrowed by weighing various criteria such as accuracy, reliability, ease of use, availability, comprehensibility, and authority.

Location and Access

Location and access is the implementation of the information seeking strategy. After deciding on an appropriate strategy, students must attempt to carry out the strategy in order to acquire the desired information resources needed to meet the defined task. This involves employing skills associated with physically finding information resources (including using access tools), and then getting to the appropriate information within a source.

Developing these abilities is the focus of most traditional library skills instructional programs. Examples of location and access skills include:

- use of access tools

- arrangement of materials in library media centers

- parts of a book

- strategies for searching an online catalog.

The Big Six Skills approach recognizes the value of students learning location and access skills. However, these skills do not receive the emphasis that they do in traditional library curricula.   Too often, the major portion of library media specialists' instructional efforts involves teaching specific skills associated with using the *Readers' Guide*, the catalog, or other access tools. While students may successfully learn how to use specific tools, at least in the short-term, they lack an understanding of how these skills transfer to other situations or fit into a more general information seeking and use conceptualization. Library personnel at high school and university levels frequently complain that students are unable to use simple access tools - even though they probably received repeated instruction in elementary, middle, and junior high schools!

The Big Six Skills approach presents location and access within a broad, problem-solving context. Students learn that *getting to* the material follows logically after deciding what it is you wish to find and where you might find it. They also learn that it is necessary to use certain tools and system commands to locate and access information. Whether they receive specific instruction on how to use a particular source will depend on the overall time available for instruction. Instruction in specifics comes after instruction in the overall information problem-solving process.

Use of Information

Use of information encompasses the set of skills that students apply to a single information source. Once students are able to locate and access a source, they must be able to interact with the information (e.g., read, view, listen), decide what is valuable for the particular situation, and somehow extract the information (e.g., take notes, copy, cite).

Information use also involves notetaking, bibliographic format, interviewing, and other techniques that are used to properly excerpt material for future use. For some information needs, extracting information from sources is a simple process. For others, it requires extensive effort.

Obviously, many of the specific skills that students apply to information use are developed in the various subject areas:

- Reading, listening, and viewing are the major aspects of the language arts curriculum.

- Map reading is part of the social studies effort.

- Understanding and interpreting graphs is a concern in mathematics.

- Observation and measurement are important elements of science curricula.

- Computer use may be in all of these subjects and/or the content of a separate course of study.

The library media instructional effort can serve to (a) integrate diverse skills, (b) reinforce the need to learn these skills, and (c) show how to apply these skills to using various information sources. The library media program can also remediate group or individual deficiences and coordinate efforts to work on certain skills.

Synthesis

Synthesis is the application of all information to the defined task. As such, synthesis encompasses the restructuring or repackaging of information into new or different formats to meet the requirements of the task as defined.

For a simple task (e.g., finding the answer to a simple question like "What is the capital of Montana?"), synthesis is a matter of communicating the information in an appropriate manner – including a notation about the source of the information (e.g., *Goode's World Atlas*, my Uncle Keith). While noting the source may not be essential for a particular task, it is important that students develop the habit. Proper citing of sources should be required at every opportunity – including homework.

For complex tasks (e.g., creating a report, paper, or project), synthesis is a major undertaking that usually involves subject area teachers as well as library media specialists. Combining information from different sources, selecting appropriate presentation formats, and effectively communicating an idea that meets the initially defined task are all significant concerns within the synthesis skill area.

Evaluation

Evaluation is an easily defined critical element of the Big Six Skills. Evaluation is the examination and assessment of the information problem-solving process with regard to how *effectively* and *efficiently* the task was carried out.

In information problem-solving, the primary evaluation concern is whether or not the task, as defined, has been completed. In other words:

- Was the information problem solved?

- Was the need met?

- Was the decision made?

- Was the situation resolved?

- Does the product satisfy the requirements as originally defined?

When the answer is *no* (such as when the project or report is incomplete), it is necessary to go back and re-define the task and re-initiate the Big Six Skills process.

Evaluation also involves reflecting on the efficiency of the information problem-solving process. Students can accomplish this aspect of evaluation by considering such issues as the amount of time spent on activities which were specifically useful to meet the task or whether the amount of time needed to complete a task was miscalculated. When students consider the efficiency aspect of evaluation, it gives them insight into their personal information problem-solving style. Students' awareness of their strengths and weaknesses can lead, with instructional intervention, to overall improvements in their ability to solve future information problems.

The Big Six Skills, by definition, requires an evaluation of the product and the process. Students interact with subject area teachers and library media personnel in examining (a) the degree to which the original task, as defined, was met and (b) the efficiency of the entire information problem-solving process. Students learn to appraise their expertise at solving information problems in order to recognize skill areas that need review and remediation.

Evaluation may include a combination of internal and external measures. Internal evaluation is from the students' perspective: how they think they are doing when using the library media center and other resources to solve information problems. External evaluation includes feedback from the library media specialist, the content area teacher, or from other students.

Formal and informal measures are available for both internal and external evaluation. Formal measures include evaluation based on specific requirements, tests or timed trials. Informal measures include a diary of the research experience, a conversation with the teacher or library media specialist, or a group discussion of successful approaches. The point of evaluation should be to determine students' proficiency at the entire information problem-solving process, and the degree to which the original task, as defined, was met.

BASIC THEMES OF THE BIG SIX SKILLS INFORMATION PROBLEM-SOLVING APPROACH

The Big Six Skills represents a departure from traditional approaches to library & information skills instruction in its scope, articulation, and emphasis. These differences translate into discernible themes:

The Big Six Skills is a general approach to information problem-solving that can be applied to any information problem situation.

While consistent with the approach to research process strategies taken by others (e.g., Kuhlthau, 1989, Pitts and Stripling, 1988), the Big Six Skills approach is not just limited to those situations that require students to write a research paper or report. The Big Six Skills can be used in any situation that involves information problem-solving. For example,

In school settings:

- completing homework assignments

- studying for a test

- deciding which after-school club to join

- writing a senior thesis

- answering essay questions.

Beyond school:

- deciding what to do on Friday night

- finding out if Jane really likes me

- learning more about favorite musicians, actors, or sports figures

- discovering where to get tickets to see a popular music group

- deciding how to earn extra money.

This broad applicability makes it easy to develop the Big Six Skills in conjunction with almost any school or personal needs situation and facilitates integration with classroom curriculum. Library media specialists are able to motivate students by combining Big Six Skills instruction with topics in the curriculum and personal life situations.

The Big Six Skills is a critical thinking hierarchy.

As explained in *Curriculum Initiative*, a library & information skills curriculum based on the Big Six Skills links information problem-solving and critical thinking. The level of cognitive development is an important concern in a Big Six Skills approach. For example, simply "knowing that the *Readers' Guide to Periodical Literature* exists" represents a relatively low level of cognition. Being able to "use the *Readers' Guide* as a tool" represents a higher level, and "incorporating knowledge and use of the *Readers' Guide* within an overall problem-solving strategy" represents an even higher level.

Most traditional library skills curricula center on knowledge and understanding of sources, the lower cognitive levels. From a critical thinking perspective, it is important to go beyond knowledge and use of particular sources so that students have the ability to manipulate information.

Information processes that represent these increasingly higher levels of cognition are listed in figure 1.2. By focusing on the full range of skills needed to solve information problems, the Big Six Skills approach is able to fulfill the need to incorporate higher levels of thinking as part of library & information skills instruction. A more complete explanation of the hierarchical, critical thinking skills aspect of the Big Six Skills Curriculum can be found in *Curriculum Initiative: An Agenda and Strategy for Library Media Programs* (Eisenberg & Berkowitz, 1988).

Figure 1.2: Information Processes

Process	Cognitive Level
• Identify information needs	• Knowledge
• Explain the relationship between information resources and their appropriateness in solving specific information problems	• Comprehension
• Select appropriate information resources from a range of options	• Application
• Examine elements and see relationships within and among information resources	• Analysis
• Restructure and communicate information	• Synthesis
• Make judgments about information in relation to specific information needs	• Evaluation

The Big Six Skills approach is basic and transferable.

As previously stressed, the Big Six Skills approach is applicable to any information problem or decision-making situation. This is one of the key differences between the Big Six Skills approach and process models that center on the research process. The *classic* library assignment is the report or research paper. While papers and reports are certainly important and easily coordinated with library & information skills instruction, too many of the same type of assignments tend to overwhelm or bore students.

One solution for over-assigning research papers is to vary the required product. Students can do physical projects, demonstrations, live or video presentations. Another variation is to have students apply the Big Six Skills to everyday information problems, needs, and situations. This helps students make the connection between what they do in school and *real life*. Young people don't always apply skills learned from schoolwork to their homes and personal lives. With the Big Six Skills approach, they can, and this fosters interest and motivates students.

The Big Six Skills is also applicable across grade levels and throughout life. Elementary school students have information problems; so do secondary school students and college students. Adults also have information problems in work situations and in their personal lives. The systematic Big Six Skills approach is useful for solving information problems at any level.

Information problem-solving is not always a linear, step-by-step process.

The Big Six Skills process is generally presented as following a logical sequence from task definition through synthesis and evaluation. However, as with most human processes, information problem-solving does not always take place in a straightforward manner. The Big Six Skills approach recognizes this by promoting independent competence in each skill area. The Big Six Skills also accommodates branching or jumping out of sequence. In practice, this happens most often when students realize that they need to go back and do more work in a prior step, for example:

- A student is writing a report on the planet Saturn. After considering different strategies for finding information, she decides to check for books in the nonfiction area. Moving to location and access, she uses the online catalog to get the call number for books on the planets. There is only one in the library media center, but she finds that the book is not on the shelf. What now? It's time to go back and reconsider information seeking strategies.

- A group has finished collecting information for compiling a community resources database. They are already to the point of building the database (a synthesis skill), but realize that they forgot to note the source and date for each entry. They decide to go back to the original sources and write down the required information (an information use action).

- A student is taking notes for a paper on J.D. Salinger. Almost all of the available information resources are works of literary criticism of individual stories. The student is confused about what he is actually trying to accomplish. He decides that before going any further with note-taking (information use), he had better go back and clarify what he is trying to accomplish (task definition).

This *looping back* is very typical of information problem-solving and should be encouraged. The basic Big Six Skills graphic (see figure 1.1) is designed to capture the feedback nature of the process.

The Big Six Skills approach does not require all students to do things in exactly the same way. The Big Six Skills encourages recognition of differences in personal style and offers alternative paths to the same end.

Not everyone approaches an information problem in the same way. Irving (1986) describes Pask's categories for information seeking and use. A *holist* will systematically survey all possible information resources, select those that are high priorities, and then work through each one. A *serialist* becomes aware of a source, finds it, uses it, and then goes on to the next one. When serialists think they have enough, they quit. Pask postulates that mismatches between teacher and learner styles may account for some learning problems. McKenney and Keen (as described in Ewing, 1977) report similar differences in *systematic* and *intuitive* information gathering and problem-solving styles.

One way to deal with varying styles is to help students find out more about their tendencies and build upon them. All successful problem-solvers still employ each of the Big Six Skills. However, individuals may differ in terms of:

- time spent on each skill

- method of accomplishing each skill

- order of skills

- general strategy employed.

A *systematic* problem-solver, for example, tends to be well-organized and approaches problems with a certain strategy. The *intuitive* person is less calculating, and may use a more meandering approach. Similarly, the *holist* generally works in a *top-down*, hierarchical fashion, while the *serialist* operates in a linear, sequential manner.

As part of the *evaluation* skill, students are encouraged to reflect on their own styles and determine whether they are successful information problem-solvers. Students learn to recognize their own tendencies and strategies. Sometimes just being aware of alternative styles helps to improve overall problem-solving competence. In addition, students may discover that they need to focus special attention on improving one or two specific skill areas.

The Big Six Skills approach also accommodates the emotional or affective side of information problem-solving. Kuhlthau (1987) has determined that identifiable emotional states (e.g., uncertainty, optimism, frustration) accompany various stages of the library research process. Students who are aware that others share similar emotions and have a strategy for solving information problems are often better able to cope with emotional and procedural difficulties.

The Big Six Skills provides a broad structure for library & information skills curricula. Existing scope and sequence approaches are easily adapted to the Big Six Skills structure.

The Big Six Skills provides a broad framework for information problem-solving. It is designed to be applicable in all library media situations by allowing for differences in emphasis based upon local needs. One school library media specialist may choose to highlight and provide in-depth development of information seeking strategies; another may determine that students need special work on synthesis. The challenge is to discover local needs and implement programs that emphasize particular skills within an overall information problem-solving context. In this way, the Big Six Skills approach builds on existing strengths of library media programs. Adopting the Big Six Skills does not involve abandoning all existing efforts and starting over. Rather, it requires restructuring skills, objectives, units, and lessons within the Big Six Skills framework. Most of Chapter 4 is concerned with how to adapt, revise, and add to existing library media instructional efforts in order to be consistent with the Big Six Skills approach.

Normally, when library media specialists speak in terms of *scope* and *sequence* they mean the scope of skills to be covered and a K-12 sequence for these skills. The Big Six Skills approach also deals with scope and sequence. In the Big Six Skills approach, however, the scope and sequence center on the the information problem-solving process.

The scope covers the Big Six Skills - the six skills areas that comprise the information problem-solving process and a range of specific competencies under each. More details on these specific competencies are offered in the next chapter.

The scope also refers to (a) the level of specificity that is developed given the constraints of available time (e.g., student time, instructional time, planning time) and available resources and (b) the degree to which the library & information skills effort is integrated into the overall school curriculum.

The sequence in a Big Six Skills approach is the information problem-solving sequence. Students normally work from Task Definition through Evaluation. However, the exact sequence is not rigid. Sequence also refers to the increasing sophistication of effort, K through 12 and beyond. The Big Six Skills approach promotes increasing complexity while providing consistency of approach and terminology across grade levels.

The Big Six Skills approach is ideal for integrating skills instruction with subject area curriculum.

The Big Six Skills is easily adaptable to any situation. The goal is to develop the full range of skills over a number of years. The first objective is to help students gain an understanding of the overall information problem-solving process; the second objective is to increase their competence in specific skill areas.

Therefore, for a given grade level, the strategy is to look at the actual classroom curriculum to determine those subject area units that are best suited to developing (a) overall problem-solving abilities and (b) proficiency in one or two specific Big Six Skills. Curriculum mapping is one technique for documenting the actual curriculum of classes; collecting assignments is another way to find out what is going on. Experience has shown that once curriculum data are collected, it is relatively easy to uncover curriculum units appropriate for coordination with Big Six Skills instruction. There is no single *right* unit for teaching a particular skill. Most often, there are several units that will do. The task for library media specialists is to analyze the subject area curriculum in relation to the Big Six Skills. The skills instructional program can then be planned and laid out in a matrix and yearly timeline (see *Curriculum Initiative*, Chapter 7, for more detail on how to accomplish this).

While each instructional opportunity should reinforce the broad information problem-solving process, specific units and lessons should seek to develop only one or two of the Big Six Skills. Again, the goal is to develop the full range of skills over a number of years. Emphasis on particular skill areas in one year can be complemented by emphasis in other areas during later years.

Furthermore, some redundancy should be built into the overall library & information skills program. Each of the Big Six Skills should be addressed a number of times from kindergarten through grade 12, in a range of different subject areas. For example, for task definition:

- Third-grade students required to draw a realistic picture of an animal are able to select an animal and recognize that they need to find a picture of that animal to complete the assignment.

- Eighth-grade students working on an earth science lab realize that they need more information on the geologic history of the local area.

- Seniors writing literary research papers learn to write a thesis sentence and discover the kind of evidence required to support their thesis.

In this way, students learn the skill of task definition through a variety of curriculum-based experiences. Across the grades, students are able to develop increasing sophistication in specific skills - always within a consistent, Big Six Skills framework.

The Big Six Skills approach is an information problem-solving process.

Every day, people are faced with numerous information needs, some more important than others. Consciously or not, individuals undertake an active process to meet those needs. The Big Six Skills approach seeks to sharpen students' information problem-solving ability by teaching a specific process. This effort to educate students to use a process approach gives them a reliable way to meet information needs. Students will apply the Big Six Skills process consciously or unconsciously depending on the complexity or newness of the problem.

Meeting an information need in any situation involves working through the Big Six problem-solving process. A library & information skills instructional program based on the Big Six Skills Curriculum stresses the idea that it is appropriate and vital to think in terms of the Big Six Skills information problem-solving process any time an information need exists. The Big Six Skills becomes part of the student's *bag of tricks*, available for use whenever he or she is confronted with information problems.

Competence in information problem-solving is developed through a series of instructional experiences. The Big Six Skills can be introduced, reviewed, remediated or practiced as individual skills, in a variety of combinations, or as a total problem-solving methodology.

The pervading goals of instruction are to have students recognize the information aspects of problem situations and to realize that they can and do use the Big Six Skills to successfully resolve these problem situations.

The Big Six Skills approach is a top-down approach.

A *top-down approach* means focusing on the *big picture* before concentrating on details. For example, in a Big Six Skills instructional situation, students should be aware of the broad, overall problem-solving process before turning to specific skills or tasks. In teaching an integrated unit, the library media specialist or teacher may stress a particular skill. However, students must always be reminded how the particular skill fits into the overall process.

From a top-down perspective, the Big Six Skills curriculum can be considered in terms of 3 levels, from broad to specific:

Level 1:   The general, information problem-solving level

Level 2:   The Big Six Skills (as described above)

Level 3:   Further articulation of the Big Six Skills; specific components that comprise each of the Big Six Skills.

The levels are highly useful for planning the overall library & information skills program as well as for developing specific units and lessons.

Specific instructional experiences (lessons and activities) can be provided to develop understanding and competence on all of these levels. These implementation activities provide opportunities for students to learn how to recognize and consider information problems and how to apply the Big Six Skills approach to solving those problems.

The three levels and implementation activities will be explained in more detail in the next chapter.

Chapter 2
The Big Six Skills Expanded

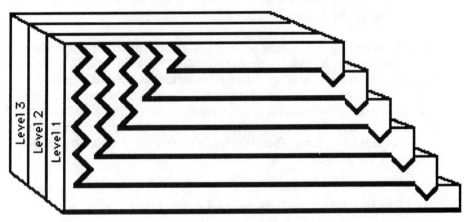

Figure 2.1: The Three Levels

INTRODUCTION

A library & information skills curriculum provides the framework from which school library media specialists meet their instructional responsibility to foster lifelong learning in their students. Library media specialists do this by teaching students to effectively and efficiently meet information needs. The Big Six Skills approach to library & information skills curriculum accomplishes this purpose.

The intent of this book, and in particular this chapter, is to articulate the full range of library & information skills associated with the information problem-solving approach of the Big Six Skills.

As noted in Chapter 1, a fundamental aspect of the Big Six Skills approach is its top-down structure. Top-down means the organization of concepts from broad to narrow, or general to specific. From an instructional perspective this means focusing on broad concepts first, and then shifting to the instruction of specific skills. When presenting the Big Six Skills to library media specialists at conferences and in-service workshops, as well as to students in elementary, secondary and university situations, we find it useful to explain the Big Six Skills in both broader and narrower terms.

The Big Six Skills approach is unique in that it is comprised of the skills necessary to solve all information-centered problems, and make information-centered decisions. Within the subtle simplicity of the design of the Big Six lies a complex array of levels of specificity and description that enhance the usability of the Big Six Skills in all learning situations, and at all levels of learning. In practice, school library media specialists may stress one level more than another.

The problem-solving process and its levels of complexity establish the inner structure of a curriculum based on the Big Six Skills. The levels of skills, Level 1 to Level 3, help students develop lifelong competencies as information problem-solvers and decision-makers. The hierarchy of skills, or levels of specificity, help students establish an information problem-solving pattern. These skills can be associated with levels of students' independence, and, therefore, impact on students' potential for success. What follows is a more detailed explanation of the levels of the Big Six Skills.

THE LEVELS OF THE BIG SIX SKILLS APPROACH

Level 1: A process approach to solving information problems

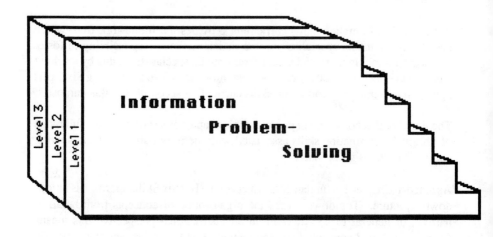

The Big Six Skills is a set of skills that provides a strategy for effectively and efficiently meeting information needs. This is the umbrella concept under which all of the other levels are presented, and under which all of the skills can be categorized. At this level students are taught that information problems exist, and to recognize when they have an information problem to be solved.

Level 1 is the broadest possible level at which to consider information problems. Working at Level 1 means recognizing that it is appropriate to use a general problem-solving process to solve all information problems.

Figure 2.2: Level 1: Information Problem-Solving

Whenever students are faced with an information problem (or with making a decision that is based on information), they can use a systematic, problem-solving process.

Library media specialists who are only able to meet with students for a short period of time, or once in an entire school year, would stress this first level of the Big Six Skills. Rather than an orientation to locating things in the library media center, the library media specialist would explain a process approach and work through examples of its application in a variety of situations – school and real world. The goals at level 1 are to teach students to be able to:

- realize that information problems are best solved systematically and logically

- recognize the information aspects of problems, tasks, and decisions.

Level 2: The Big Six Skills

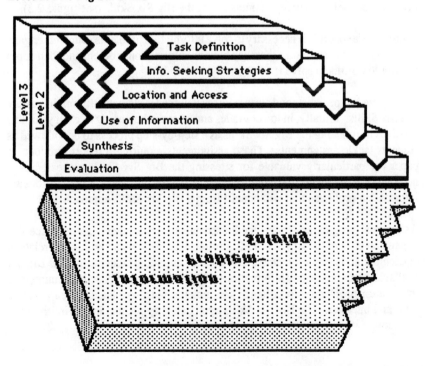

Figure 2.3: Level 2: The Big Six Skills

1. Task Definition:	determining the purpose and need for information
2. Information Seeking Strategies:	examining alternative approaches to acquiring the appropriate information to meet defined tasks
3. Location and Access:	locating information sources and information within sources
4. Use of Information:	using a source to gain information
5. Synthesis:	integrating information drawn from a range of sources
6. Evaluation:	making judgments based on a set of criteria

One level below the conceptual problem-solving umbrella is the general information problem-solving strategy comprised of the Big Six Skills (see figure 2.3).

Each of these six skills is necessary to solve information problems. Students engage level 2 when they recognize that they have an information problem and then apply the Big Six Skills to solve it.

Library media specialists and classroom teachers can systematically emphasize the Big Six Skills. Initially, in lower grades and/or at the beginning of each year, this involves introducing the Big Six Skills as a step-by-step process to be followed as students tackle assignments. Those assignments requiring a report, product, or paper are particularly valuable for stressing the Big Six Skills process. Even homework assignments that require students to simply answer a set of questions are information problems that will benefit from a Big Six Skills approach.

As the year progresses, library media specialists and teachers can reinforce and expand on each of the Big Six Skills through exercises and activities that relate to curriculum units. Reinforcement also means reminding students that the Big Six Skills can be applied to any information problem. Students are faced with numerous information problems, most often as assignments, but also related to their personal lives and interests. The Big Six Skills approach is applicable in any information situation.

Level 3: Components of the Big Six Skills

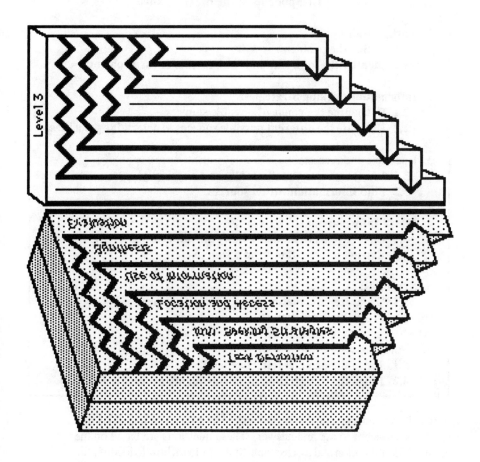

There are two specific, detailed components under each of the Big Six Skills. These singular, easily identified information acts help students to understand the specific meanings of each of the Big Six Skills (see figure 2.4). The component level is also important to library media specialists and teachers because it focuses attention on detailed information activities that are easily taught and implemented in conjunction with subject area content.

Figure 2.4: Level 3: Components of the Big Six Skills

1. Task Definition:
   1.1 Define the problem.
   1.2 Identify the information requirements of the problem.

2. Information Seeking Strategies:
   2.1 Determine the range of possible sources.
   2.2 Evaluate the different possible sources to determine priorities.

3. Location and Access:
   3.1 Locate sources (intellectually and physically).
   3.2 Find information within sources.

4. Use of Information:
   4.1 Engage (e.g., read, hear, view) the information in a source.
   4.2 Extract information from a source.

5. Synthesis:
   5.1 Organize information from multiple sources.
   5.2 Present information.

6. Evaluation:
   6.1 Judge the product (effectiveness).
   6.2 Judge the information problem-solving process (efficiency).

Level 3 components can also be thought of as a series of questions that students can learn to ask and answer. These questions are based on the skills of identification and assessment. Students learn how to identify the need and assess the degree to which that need was met at each of step in the information problem-solving process.

Level 3 Components as Questions:

Task Definition:
> What is the problem to be solved?
> What information is needed in order to solve the problem?

Information Seeking Strategies:
> What are all possible sources of information?
> What are the best of all the possibilities?

Location and Access:
    Where are these sources?
    Where is the information within each source?

Use of Information:
    What information does the source provide?
    What specific information is worth applying to the task?

Synthesis:
    How does the information from all sources fit together?
    How is the information best presented?

Evaluation:
    Was the problem solved?
    If the problem had to be solved again, what would be done differently?

Level 3 components represent unique abilities that contribute to a student's overall problem-solving effectiveness. Library media specialists can work with classroom teachers to identify opportunities for emphasizing and developing these skills components. For example, in working with students, the library media specialist may discover a gap in 8th-grade students' abilities to organize information from multiple sources. To address this, the library media specialist should review the grade 8 curriculum to discover subject area units and assignments that are particularly suited to working on this skill, for example:

- an American history assignment to create a 1920s newspaper

- a guidance unit on careers

- a science lab involving making a weather chart comparing data provided by three different sources (e.g., radio weather reports, personal observation, and newspapers)

- a language arts unit on making a case in argumentative essays.

In this way, instruction is focused on a specific level 3 component *and* directly linked to the actual curriculum of the school.

BIG SIX SKILLS IMPLEMENTATION ACTIVITIES

As stressed throughout this book and in *Curriculum Initiative*, all instruction in library & information skills should be integrated with subject area curricula. An effective way to accomplish this integration is to find opportunities within existing or planned classroom units and lessons that are directly related to the Big Six Skills. These curriculum-based opportunities then become Big Six Skills *implementation activities.*

Implementation activities may relate to any of the levels of the Big Six Skills Curriculum. For example:

- An exercise on using earth science reference tables represents the level 3 skill of engaging information in a source.

- Developing an awareness of information problems and problem-solving by having students keep a one-day log of information problems and the steps taken to resolve the problems is a broad, level 1 concern.

- Giving students three critical reviews of a film to be combined and presented in a single article, matches the level 2 skill of synthesis.

Regardless of the level of specificity, implementation activities need to be presented within a top-down context. That is, students should be aware of where a specific activity fits in the Big Six Skills hierarchy. If the activity relates to a level 3 component, the student should understand its relationship to the broader level 2 Big Six Skill as well as to the overall information problem-solving process (level 1). Conversely, if the activity relates solely to the broad level 1, students should still be aware that information problem-solving consists of six basic skills (level 2s) and a range of skills (level 3s) under each of the Big Six Skills.

The key to implementation is *action* and implementation activities represent the action part of the library & information skills instructional program. Students, library media specialists and teachers are actively engaged in endeavors designed to develop students' information problem-solving skills. Skills instruction is accomplished through a series of curriculum-based implementation activities that develop a range of understandings and skills from level 1 (the general skill of information problem-solving) to level 2 (the Big Six Skills) to level 3 (specific components of the Big Six Skills).

Few library media specialists receive special training in recognizing opportunities for information skills instruction within existing curriculum. However, it is possible to develop and improve one's abilities:

- to identify curriculum units and lessons that are suited to library & information skills instruction

- to match curriculum activities with the Big Six Skills (at all three levels)

- to design curriculum-based implementation activities for teaching the Big Six Skills (at all three levels).

Most of the remainder of this book is devoted to helping to improve these abilities through explanations, exercises, and examples. The next section provides some examples of implementation activities associated with each of the three levels.

Examples for Level 1: Information Problem-Solving

Whenever students are faced with an information problem (or with making a decision that is based on information), they can use a systematic, problem-solving process.

- Create a flowchart of the information problem-solving process taken to deal with an information problem in [any subject area].

- Compare the approach taken to complete nightly homework in math with the Big Six Skills approach. First list the steps taken to complete homework and then compare them to the steps in the Big Six Skills.

- List opportunities to use the information problem-solving process.

Examples for Level 2: The Big Six Skills

1. Task Definition: determining the purpose and need for information.

- Determine what is required in an assignment.

- Determine the order of tasks and the timeline required to do a video production.

2. Information Seeking Strategies: examining alternative approaches to acquiring the appropriate information to meet defined tasks.

- Brainstorm what sources can and should be used to find out about Elvis Presley.

- From all the possible subject reference works in the library media center, decide which ones are likely to provide information on sports personalities.

3. Location and Access: Locating information sources and information within sources.

- Get a journal issue from the periodical room, and turn to the correct page number for the relevant article.

- Go to the public library and take out a book on a U.S. president.

4. Use of Information: using a source to gain information.

- View a videotape on earthquakes and outline the major points.

- Examine the back-of-the book glossary to see if a term is included, and if so write down the definition.

5. Synthesis: integrating information drawn from a range of sources.

- Make an outline (using information from multiple sources) for a report on a topic.

- Prepare a video production on clubs in the school.

6. Evaluation: making judgments based on a set of criteria.

- Determine "why didn't I get an A on that report."

- Decide whether or not an assignment is fully completed.

Examples for Level 3: Components of the Big Six Skills

Task Definition

1.1 Define the problem

- Outline the steps for preparing for physical education class and note if any information is required for any step.

- Determine whether any of the activities for a science lab have some information requirement.

1.2 Identify the information requirements of the problem.

- For each information-related activity in the same science lab, note whether it involves location and access, information use, or synthesis.

- Realize that the assigment requires both looking at and labeling a map.

Information Seeking Strategies

2.1 Determine the range of possible sources

- List where to find literary criticism information.

- Inventory all the computer resources available in the school.

2.2 Evaluate the different possible sources to determine priorities

- Decide whether to ask an expert or use a reference book.

- Decide whether it is OK to use an encyclopedia for an assignment.

Location and Access

3.1 Locate sources (intellectually and physically)

- Find a particular book on the shelf.

- Draw and label a map of the library media center.

3.2 Find information within sources

- Look up an article in the SIRS' *Energy* series.

- Find an article on the current rock music scene using a periodical index on CD-ROM.

Use of Information

4.1 Engage (e.g., read, hear, view) the information in a source

- Scan a book to determine its usefulness.

- Listen to an audiocassette of *Tale of Two Cities*.

4.2 Extract information from a source

- Take notes on bibliographic information for later use.

- Take notes on a magazine article.

Synthesis

5.1 Organize information from multiple sources

- Create a database on the major cities of the Midwest.

- Put note cards (from multiple sources) in a logical order.

5.2 Present information

- Create a printout from a database.

- Draw and label a map of Africa.

Evaluation

6.1 Judge the product (effectiveness)

- Set criteria for judging anti-smoking posters.

- Determine whether the information need as originally defined is met.

6.2 Judge the information problem-solving process (efficiency)

- Determine the degree to which notetaking techniques are working.

- State what you would do differently next time.

For each implementation activity, the appropriate level of instruction is determined by students' needs and degree of proficiency. The design of a library & information skills instructional sequence must consider whether students:

- will be taught new skills

- will review previously taught skills

- will be remediated to correct any misunderstanding

- will be reinforced to become more competent.

Overall skills development calls for flexible and creative approaches to integrated instruction. Careful consideration should be given to both the subject objectives of the curricular unit and lesson(s) and the Big Six Skills objectives. In order to cover all the Big Six Skills, it is necessary to:

- vary the emphasis of instruction from one integrated unit or lesson to another

- implement the Big Six Skills within the context of the school's overall curriculum

- explain each of the Big Six Skills and components within the context of the information problem-solving process regardless of the skill level.

Students should always be able to state how a particular action fits into the overall Big Six Skills framework. How do particular actions help them to resolve their information problems? They should also be able to discuss the value of the Big Six Skills to their success. Library media specialists and teachers must continually reinforce this contextual approach.

CONCLUSION

Whether viewed as a simple but effective curriculum design, or a complex set of skills requiring careful monitoring, the bottom line is that the Big Six Skills works. Library media specialists are able to present a unified set of essential information skills. Students are able to quickly grasp the overall problem-solving strategy and learn specific competencies. Teachers see the value and ease of integrating these transferable information skills within the content of their curriculum.

The goal of this chapter was to carefully present the hierarchy that exists within the Big Six Skills approach. This global view detailed the set of skills that comprise the information problem-solving process put forth as a series of ordered levels and sample implementation activities. What is ultimately important to remember is that a library & information skills curriculum based on an information problem-solving process (such as the Big Six Skills) provides students with transferable and generalizable skills. When students gain competency with this set of skills and abilities, they attain the capacity to become effective lifelong users of information and, in turn, acquire the capacity for lifelong learning.

Chapter 3
The Big Six Skills Developed

INTRODUCTION

The previous chapter concluded with an explanation of implementation activities, those specific curriculum-related actions that require students to apply various levels of the Big Six Skills. The purpose of this chapter is to further explore the connection between the Big Six Skills and curriculum implementation activities.

In order to truly integrate information skills instruction with the classroom curriculum, it is necessary to match existing curriculum activities with related Big Six Skills. Successful accomplishment of this matching task requires being able to (1) analyze and evaluate specific curriculum activities from an information problem-solving perspective and (2) recognize where the curriculum and the various Big Six Skills intersect.

For example, students are frequently asked to choose a topic for a paper, research report, or project. From the Big Six Skills perspective, this is defining the problem, a component of task definition. Similarly, viewing a film, listening to a tape, or reading a passage from a book all involve engaging the information in a source, which is a component of information use. By recognizing these types of connections, library media specialists can offer instruction in information problem-solving that is directly linked to the specific curriculum needs of students.

Analysis and evaluation are sophisticated processes, and first attempts to match activities and the Big Six Skills may not be easy. However, this ability can be greatly improved through practice and experience. This chapter provides two sets of exercises designed to help develop this matching ability. In a relatively short period of time, most library media specialists are able to easily recognize numerous relationships between the curriculum and the Big Six Skills. In fact, since many curriculum activities lend themselves to Big Six Skills instruction, the ultimate challenge becomes selecting from among the numerous opportunities to determine which activities will be most effective for developing specific Big Six Skills and components.

Some activities are almost always associated with certain Big Six Skills:

- Anything to do with an assignment – analyzing it, determining what is really being asked, or breaking it up into more details – usually relates to task definition.

- *Brainstorming* often involves determining all possibilities which is a component of information seeking strategies.

- *Looking something up* is a location and access activity.

- *Notetaking* is a typical activity for use of information.

- Any act of *creating* (e.g., writing, composing, painting) is synthesis.

- *Making judgments* is probably tied to evaluation.

At the same time, there is a certain degree of flexibility in interpreting a specific activity in relation to the Big Six Skills. For example, if students are asked to *make a picture book of community helpers*, it is reasonable to focus on task definition and the related components of defining the problem and identifying the information requirements of the problem. However, a library media specialist or teacher could just as easily emphasize synthesis, in terms of organizing information from multiple sources and presenting information. Exactly how some activities are used will depend on the needs of the students in relation to the overall information skills instructional effort.

The exercises that follow are offered to library media specialists and other educators who wish to sharpen their ability to match curriculum activities and Big Six Skills. The exercises are not a test of knowledge, rather they are tools to help develop analytical and recognition expertise. In completing the exercises, consider the definitions of the Big Six Skills (see figure 3.1), the logical sequence of various activities, and the common links noted immediately above.

Figure 3.1: Definitions of the Big Six Skills

1. **Task Definition:**
   1.1 **Define the problem.**
   1.2 **Identify the information requirements of the problem.**

2. **Information Seeking Strategies:**
   2.1 **Determine the range of possible sources.**
   2.2 **Evaluate the different possible sources to determine priorities.**

3. **Location and Access:**
   3.1 **Locate sources (intellectually and physically).**
   3.2 **Find information within sources.**

4. **Use of Information:**
   4.1 **Engage (e.g., read, hear, view) the information in a source.**
   4.2 **Extract information from a source.**

5. **Synthesis:**
   5.1 **Organize information from multiple sources.**
   5.2 **Present information.**

6. **Evaluation:**
   6.1 **Judge the product (effectiveness).**
   6.2 **Judge the information problem-solving process (efficiency).**

EXERCISE 1: MATCHING ACTIVITIES AND BIG SIX SKILLS

The first set of exercises offers a situation and specific curriculum activities. The goal is to match each activity with a related Big Six Skill. For each exercise, the suggested approach is to:

- Briefly review the definitions of the Big Six Skills (see figure 3.1).
- Read carefully through the description of the situation.
- Scan through all six activities.
- Try to place the activities in a logical, sequential order.
- Match all the activities to related Big Six Skills.
- Review your choices in Big Six Skills order (from Task Definition to Evaluation).
- Note your rationale for each match.

Exercise 1a. [SAMPLE]

Objectives

To match each of the activities (in the first column) with the appropriate Big Six Skill (in the second column) and explain your reasons for doing so (in the third column). There is one activity for each of the Big Six Skills.

Situation

Students in a 4th-grade class are studying dinosaurs. As part of the unit, the teacher would like each student to do one special project. The students may choose from writing a short report, making a physical model, or painting or drawing a mural.

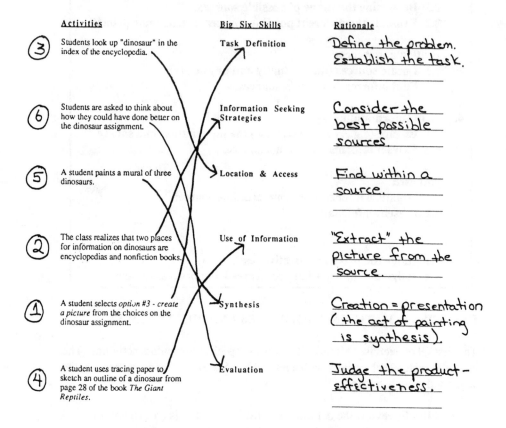

Activities

(3) Students look up "dinosaur" in the index of the encyclopedia.

(6) Students are asked to think about how they could have done better on the dinosaur assignment.

(5) A student paints a mural of three dinosaurs.

(2) The class realizes that two places for information on dinosaurs are encyclopedias and nonfiction books.

(1) A student selects *option #3 - create a picture* from the choices on the dinosaur assignment.

(4) A student uses tracing paper to sketch an outline of a dinosaur from page 28 of the book *The Giant Reptiles*.

Big Six Skills

Task Definition

Information Seeking Strategies

Location & Access

Use of Information

Synthesis

Evaluation

Rationale

Define the problem. Establish the task.

Consider the best possible sources.

Find within a source.

"Extract" the picture from the source.

Creation = presentation (the act of painting is synthesis).

Judge the product – effectiveness.

Exercise 1b.

Objectives

To match each of the activities (in the first column) with the appropriate Big Six Skill (in the second column) and explain your reasons for doing so (in the third column). There is one activity for each of the Big Six Skills.

Situation

Students in a 6th-grade class* are working on vocabulary. The students are given a list of 15 terms to define in their own words. The teacher requires that students note the source for each definition, including page numbers if appropriate.

Activities	Big Six Skills	Rationale
Students use the guide words in a dictionary.	Task Definition	_____ _____ _____
Through discussion, the class determines the type of dictionary needed.	Information Seeking Strategies	_____ _____ _____
Each student critiques the amount of time it took to complete the assignment.	Location & Access	_____ _____ _____
A student recognizes that the key to the assignment is stating the definitions in her own words.	Use of Information	_____ _____ _____
Students make a final alphabetized list of the terms with defintions and notations on sources.	Synthesis	_____ _____ _____
Students take notes from the dictionary on the definition of each term.	Evaluation	_____ _____ _____

Answers and discussion are in Appendix A.

---

*Although this situation is presented in a grade 6 context, it is common to many grade levels. If useful, adjust the activities to better simulate your own situation.

Exercise 1c.

Objectives

To match each of the activities (in the first column) with the appropriate Big Six Skill (in the second column) and explain your reasons for doing so (in the third column). There is one activity for each of the Big Six Skills.

Situation

Students in 11th-grade social studies are required to complete a timeline.* Given a list of 10 dates, they are to determine what happened on that date, whether the date is truly significant in U.S. history, and if so, to place the event on the proper place on the timeline.

Activities	Big Six Skills	Rationale
Students are asked to check to see if all parts of the assignment have been completed.	Task Definition	_____ _____ _____
A student gets to the "Memorable Dates in U.S. history" section in the *World Almanac* by using the "Quick Reference Index;" another gets there through the "General Index."	Information Seeking Strategies	_____ _____ _____
A student reads the entry for a given date and makes a note about what happened.	Location & Access	_____ _____ _____
Through explanation, the class realizes that the assignment really has three parts.	Use of Information	_____ _____ _____
A student puts the significant events on the timeline.	Synthesis	_____ _____ _____
After talking with the library media specialist, two students decide that an almanac is probably a better source than their history textbook.	Evaluation	_____ _____ _____

Answers and discussion are in Appendix A.

---

*Again, this situation and assignment are common to many grade levels.

EXERCISE 2: GENERATING ACTIVITIES FOR A SITUATION

The second set of exercises moves from the Big Six Skills to specific curriculum activities. The goal is to provide possible activities for each of the Big Six Skills. For each situation, the suggested approach is to:

- Read carefully through the description of the situation. Consider how the situation could be used to develop student competence in information problem-solving.

- Make note of any initial reactions.

- Scan through the definitions of the Big Six Skills.

- Consider the examples.

- Brainstorm possible activities related to each of the Big Six Skills.

- For each of the Big Six Skills, select two possible activities and record in the space provided.

- When completed, assess and revise as deemed desirable.

Exercise 2a: [SAMPLE]

Objectives

For the given curriculum situation, describe one or two activities that relate to each of the Big Six Skills.

Situation

A 7th-grade health class is studying nutrition. Through lecture/discussion/video/films the teacher introduces the major nutritional topics. These topics will be evaluated through an end-of-unit test. In addition, the students are broken into groups of 4 and are required to do a visual or audio nutrition project. Examples of projects are a 60-second TV or radio commercial, a brochure, or a poster.

Task Definition

1.1 Define the problem
1.2 Identify the information requirements of the problem

The teacher talks about working in groups and decision-making. After determining the topic and format, students lay out the tasks, timeframe, and divide up responsibilities.

Information Seeking Strategies

2.1 Determine the range of possible sources
2.2 Evaluate the different possible sources to determine priorities

The library media specialist leads a class discussion on text and human sources for the topic. In groups, the students decide which sources are priorities.

Location and Access

3.1 Locate sources (physically and intellectually)
3.2 Find information within sources

Students go in groups to the LMC, get materials, and return to class. Students take out magazines overnight.

Use of Information

4.1 Engage (e.g., read, hear, view) the information in a source
4.2 Extract information from a source

Students take notes on the information from the sources.

Synthesis

5.1 Organize information from multiple sources
5.2 Present information

Each student explains to the group what he/she has found. The group decides which information to use in the project.

Evaluation

6.1 Judge the product (effectiveness)
6.2 Judge the information problem-solving process (efficiency)

Each group determines whether they have enough information or need more.

NOTES:

Exercise 2b.

Objective

For the given curriculum situation, describe one or two activities that relate to each of the Big Six Skills.

Situation

A 12th-grade economics class is studying large corporations and how to actually determine how well a company is doing. Students are to choose a company, write a profile of the company and discuss the relative value of different sources of information about the company.

Task Definition

1.1 Define the problem
1.2 Identify the information requirements of the problem

The library media specialist discusses (with the full class) the type of information needed – primary information from the company, and secondary information from analysts and others.

Information Seeking Strategies

2.1 Determine the range of possible sources
2.2 Evaluate the different possible sources to determine priorities

The students ask questions about various business-oriented information resources – print and computer.

Location and Access

3.1 Locate sources (physically and intellectually)
3.2 Find information within sources

Use of Information

4.1 Engage (e.g., read, hear, view) the information in a source
4.2 Extract information from a source

Synthesis

5.1 Organize information from multiple sources
5.2 Present information

Evaluation

6.1 Judge the product (effectiveness)
6.2 Judge the information problem-solving process (efficiency)

The library media specialist asks the class to discuss how difficult it was to get/use the online vs. print sources.

NOTES:

Exercise 2c.

Objective

For the given curriculum situation, describe one or two activities that relate to each of the Big Six Skills.

Situation

A 1st-grade class is studying *community* (what makes a community, people and places in their community). Each student is going to make a picture book of community helpers. Each entry in the picture book should include a picture of a community person in the appropriate setting and a sentence (or two) describing who the person is and what he or she does. The teacher gives the students information about three helpers, and the students are to add at least five on their own. The teacher also sends home an explanation sheet to parents suggesting how they can help their children.

Task Definition

1.1 Define the problem
1.2 Identify the information requirements of the problem

Information Seeking Strategies

2.1 Determine the range of possible sources
2.2 Evaluate the different possible sources to determine priorities

Location and Access

3.1 Locate sources (physically and intellectually)
3.2 Find information within sources

Use of Information

4.1 Engage (e.g., read, hear, view) the information in a source
4.2 Extract information from a source

Synthesis

5.1 Organize information from multiple sources
5.2 Present information

Evaluation

6.1 Judge the product (effectiveness)
6.2 Judge the information problem-solving process (efficiency)

NOTES:

Chapter 4
The Big Six Skills Implemented

A process for systematically implementing the overall library media program was presented in *Curriculum Initiative*. The "Six Stage Strategy" is a library media planning model that involves the following:

1. Review the existing situation
2. Define goals and objectives
3. Set up support systems
4. Conduct feasibility analysis
5. Develop plans
6. Evaluate plans and processes.

The approach of the Six Stage Strategy is consistent with most program planning models in that it follows a common cycle of information gathering, analysis, planning, and evaluation. The Six Stage Strategy was purposely designed to consider all curriculum related goals of the library media program: services as well as instruction. Since the primary concern of this book is the skills instruction program, this chapter focuses on specific acts that promote that goal. All the actions described below add to the effectiveness of the Six Stage Strategy.

The overriding task is to provide an instructional program that integrates library & information skills objectives with classroom content (see figure 4.1). This is accomplished by developing and documenting:

- library & information skills objectives

- individual class as well as subject area curriculum objectives

- general and specific plans for the integrated program.

Library & information skills instruction should always be implemented within a curriculum context. Therefore, the Big Six Skills instructional effort is most accurately represented as the intersection of library & information skills objectives and subject area curriclum objectives (again, see figure 4.1).

This chapter offers actions that fully explore each of these three essential elements for an integrated instructional effort. Together they provide the necessary foundation for an effective library & information skills program based on information problem-solving.

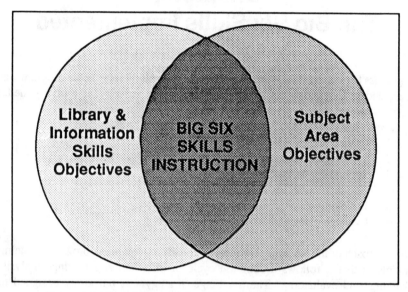

Figure 4.1: The Library & Information Skills Instructional Program

DEVELOP AND DOCUMENT
LIBRARY & INFORMATION SKILLS OBJECTIVES

Review and revise scope and sequence documents

Those readers currently working in library media programs probably recognize that many components of their present library & information skills instructional program are compatible with the Big Six Skills approach. In fact, in Chapter 1, we stated that a basic theme of the Big Six Skills curriculum is that existing curricula are easily adapted to the Big Six Skills structure.

Successful program planning begins with establishing goals and setting realistic expectations. For the library & information skills instructional program, this is accomplished by first determining the nature and scope of skills to be covered. Again, we recommend building on existing efforts by reconsidering the existing library & information skills curriculum from a Big Six Skills perspective.   The question here is, how do we accomplish this?

The most common expression of expectations for library media instructional efforts are *scope and sequence* documents. Even those readers not working as library media specialists are probably familiar with these curriculum outlines produced on the state, regional, and local levels. Figure 4.2 is an example of a typical K-12 scope and sequence, and figures 4.3 through 4.5 show the progressions from a traditional approach to an example of an approach based on information problem-solving.

As with most traditional scope and sequence documents, the scope of the curriculum presented in figure 4.2 covers the physical library media setting and content resources. This general K-12 sequence involves an increasing number of resource options as well as increasing depth, from introduced to expanded instruction. Specific items to be taught are listed independently, with little concern about need, context, or process. Those few process concerns listed (e.g., materials use and research skills), are generally reserved for the higher grade levels. Therefore, the major limitation of the curriculum is the absence of any unifying approach to meeting information needs.

This limitation can be addressed by rethinking and revising the curriculum in terms of the Big Six Skills perspective. Figure 4.3 illustrates the first phase of the revising activity. This essentially involves analyzing each item listed in the scope and sequence to determine where it might fit in the Big Six Skills framework, for example:

- *Layout of the LMC* is a location skill (component 3.1 - locate sources intellectually and physically).

- *Public Library* is part of information seeking strategy (component 2.1 - determine the range of possible sources and component 2.2 - evaluate the different possible sources to determine priorities).

- *Taking Notes* is an activity under information use (component 4.2 - extract information from a source).

In some cases, items may seem to fit into more than one of the Big Six Skills. This is particularly true for the many specific sources listed (e.g., almanacs, dictionaries, encyclopedias). If an almanac is considered within the range of sources potentially applicable to an information problem, the focus is information seeking strategies. Actually getting to the almanac and to the appropriate information in the almanac is location and access. Finally, using the almanac and extracting the relevant information involves information use. All these possibilities should be noted and considered during the revision process.

After the entire curriculum is analyzed, a working draft of a revised scope and sequence is created by organizing the items under the specific Big Six Skills (see figure 4.3). This draft is further altered by asking:

(1) Are each of the level 2 Big Six Skills covered to some degree (e.g., introduced, reviewed, or expanded) at each grade level? What level 2 and 3 skills seem to be missing?

(2) Which items may be receiving too much attention and should be altered or placed within a different context?

Figure 4.4 presents a working draft with notations relating to these two questions. Answers to question 1 are noted as *gaps*. Answers to question 2 are noted as *too much?*

Figure 4.5 is a revised scope and sequence in a Big Six Skills framework. Some of the gaps are filled and alterations made. At this point, the original grade designations are still intact. However, these may also be revised as deemed appropriate. The resulting curriculum retains some of the original emphasis, but now within a process context. For example, literature appreciation is still included, but now it is (a) noted as part of task definition, location and access, and information seeking strategies, and (b) emphasized under information use.

Determine the time available for direct instruction

As always, the amount of available time is a key determinant to meaningful ibrary & information skills instruction. When a library media specialist's time is severely limited, the emphasis and level of instruction remains at the more general levels. In a Big Six Skills context, such a limitation might translate to only focusing on the applicability of a process approach to information problem-solving (level 1) and the broad descriptions of each of the Big Six Skills (level 2).

For example, consider a situation in which direct library media specialist contact with students is limited to a few sessions each year. Even in this situation, the library media specialist can be effective by

- setting the library & information skills objectives at the more general levels

- identifying major units within the curriculum that provide opportunities to focus on these broad skills objectives

- designating relevant implementation activities

- documenting intentions through plans.

One way to expand instruction in constrained situations is to build some of the library & information skills instruction into classroom curriculum activities. True, this too requires time (for analysis of curriculum and planning and coordination with teachers) but the payoff can be well worth the effort. The curriculum review techniques described in the next section make it easier to analyze, plan, and coordinate integrated instructional efforts.

In terms of scheduling, it is certainly easier to customize and target skills instruction if library media center use is not rigidly scheduled. Flexible scheduling allows the library media program to work with student groups based on need. For example, if a class or grade requires in-depth instruction over a three-day period, that can be easily accommodated. Flexible scheduling facilitates integrated instruction by allowing the library media program to schedule intensive blocks for instruction and library media use based on major units in the curriculum. Furthermore, the library media center is always open to individual or small groups of students who have information needs arising out of classroom activities.

In a fixed schedule situation, it is still possible to provide meaningful instruction in information problem-solving. In fact, in fixed schedule situations it is even more crucial that library media specialists use every opportunity to reinforce the unifying Big Six Skills context. Library media specialists who meet with classes every week often develop a yearly program comprised of a series of instructional lessons interspersed with reading guidance, literature appreciation, and other activities. It is possible to make library & information skills instructional lessons more effective by

- linking to classroom curriculum needs

- focusing on just one of the Big Six Skills or level 3 components of one of the Big Six Skills

- always presenting the lesson within the overall Big Six Skills context.

The curriculum link insures that the library & information skills instructional effort is related to the real needs of students. Focusing on one skill narrows the scope of the lesson and helps students to develop specific competencies. Reinforcing the information problem-solving context helps students to see relationships among seemingly independent activities and encourages students to apply skills developed in one situation to others.

DOCUMENT THE EXISTING CURRICULUM OF THE SCHOOL

It is widely accepted that a key to successful library & information skills instruction is integration with classroom curriculum.   The mission of the library media program, according to *Information Power*, "is to ensure that students and staff are effective users of ideas and information." Furthermore, "achievement of this mission at both school and district levels requires: *full integration of the library media program into the curriculum*." [emphasis added] (AASL/AECT pp. 1-2)

Figure 4.2: Typical Library Skills Curriculum

	K	1	2	3	4	5	6	7	8	9	10	11	12
Organization of the LMC						*Includes orientation to the LMC*							
Layout of the LMC	I	I	I	R	R	R	R	E	E	E	E		
Shelf Arrangement		I	I	R	R	R	R	E	E	E	E		
Reference Section			I	I	R	R	R	E	E	E		E	E
Nonfiction			I	I	R	R	E	E	E	E			
Fiction			I	I	R	R	R	E	E	E	E		
Biography			I	I	R	R	E	E	E	E			
Periodicals	I	I	R	R	R	R	E	E			E	E	R
AV Materials		I	I	R	R	R	R	E	E	E	E	E	R
Equipment		I	I	R	R	R	R	E	E	E	E	E	R
Computers			I	I	R	R	R	E	E	E	E	E	E
Library Classification System					*Includes organization and arrangement*								
Catalog			I	I	R	R	R	E	E	E	E		
Dewey Decimal System			I	I	R	R	R	E	E	E	E		
Subject Headings			I	I	R	R	R	E	E	E			
Library Citizenship					*Includes policies, procedures, & expectations*								
Circulation	I	I	I	R	R	R	R	E	E	E	E	R	R
Use Areas	I	I	I	R	R	R	R	E	E	E	E	R	R
Public Library			I	I	R	R	R	E	E	E	E	R	R
Academic Libraries										I	R	E	E
Materials Use													
Parts of a Book	I	I	R	R	R	E	E	E		E			
Using Back-of-the-Book Indexes			I	I	R	R	E			E			
Using Periodical Indexes						I	I	E	E	R	E	E	
Searching via Computer								I	I	R	E	E	E
Primary/Secondary Sources						I	I	I	R	R	E	E	
Using Equipment		I	I	R	R	R	E	E	R	E			E
Research Skills													
Selecting a Topic								I	I	E	E	E	E
Using Appropriate Sources								I	I	R	E	E	E
Taking Notes								I	I	R	R	E	E
Footnotes									I	R	E	R	E
Bibliography								I	R	R	E	R	E

NOTE: ASSUMES K-6 ELEMENTARY, 7-8 OR 7-9 MIDDLE, 9-12 OR 10-12 HIGH SCHOOL

	K	1	2	3	4	5	6	7	8	9	10	11	12
Types of Resources													
Information Books			I	I	R	E	E	E	E	R	E		
Indexes							I	I	E	E	E	E	E
Dictionaries			I	I	R	R	R	R	E	R	R	E	R
Encyclopedias			I	I	R	R	E	E	R		E		
Atlases			I	I	R	R	E	E					
Almanacs						I	I	R	E	R	R	E	
Thesauri							I	I	I	R	R	E	E
Vertical File			I	I	R	R	R	R	E	R	R	E	R
Microform									I	R	R	E	E
AV Software			I	I	R	R	R	R	E	E	R	E	R
Computer Software			I	I	R	R	R	E	R	R	E	R	
Special Subject Sources													
Biographical Sources							I	I	I	R	R	E	E
Current Events Sources							I	I	I	R	R	E	E
Literary Sources							I	I	R	R	E	E	E
Arts Sources									I	R	E	E	E
Career Sources								I	R	R	E	E	E
Literature Appreciation													
Folk Tales	I	I	R	R	R	R	R	E	E	E	E		
Picture Books	I	R	R										
Poetry	I	I	R	R	R			E	E	E	E	E	E
Plays					I	I	R	E	R	R	E	E	
Mythology	I	I	R	R	R	R	R	E	E	E	E	E	E
Biography					I	R	R	E	R	R	E	R	R
Fiction				I	I	R	E	E	E	R	R	E	E
Literary Criticism								I	R	R	E	E	E

I = INSTRUCT, R=REVIEW/REINFORCE, E = EXPAND

Figure 4.3: Edited Version of Library Skills Curriculum

[Handwritten: 3.1 Location (physically + intellectually)]

	K	1	2	3	4	5	6	7	8	9	10	11	12
Organization of the LMC				*Includes orientation to the LMC*									
Layout of the LMC	I	I	I	R	R	R	R	E	E	E	E		
Shelf Arrangement	I	I	I	R	R	R	E	E	E	E			
Reference Section		I	I	R	R	R	E	E	E	E	E		
Nonfiction		I	I	R	R	E	E	E	E				
Fiction	I	I	I	R	R	E	E	E	E				
Biography		I	I	R	R	E	E	E	E				
Periodicals	I	I	R	R	R	R	E	E		E	E	R	
AV Materials	I	I	R	R	R	E	E	E	E	E	R		
Equipment	I	I	R	R	R	R	E	E	E	E	E	R	
Computers	I	I	R	R	R	E	E	E	E	E	E		

[Handwritten: → in many sections]

[Handwritten: 3.2 Access within a source (source = the nonfiction collection)]

	K	1	2	3	4	5	6	7	8	9	10	11	12
Library Classification System				*Includes organization and arrangement*									
Catalog		I	I	R	R	R	E	E	E				
Dewey Decimal System		I	I	R	R	E	E	E	E				
Subject Headings		I	I	R	R	R	E	E	E				

[Handwritten: → 4.2 Info. Use]

	K	1	2	3	4	5	6	7	8	9	10	11	12
Library Citizenship				*Includes policies, procedures, & expectations*									
Circulation	I	I	I	R	R	R	E	E	E	E	R	R	
Use Areas	I	I	I	R	R	R	E	E	E	E	R	R	
Public Library		I	I	R	R	R	E	E	E	E	R	R	
Academic Libraries										I	R	E	E

[Handwritten: Info. Seeking Strategies → 2.1 & 2.2]

[Handwritten: , - Loc & Access]

	K	1	2	3	4	5	6	7	8	9	10	11	12
Materials Use													
Parts of a Book	I	I	R	R	R	E	E	E		E			
Using Back-of-the-Book Indexes	I	I	R	R	E			E					
Using Periodical Indexes			I	I	E	E	R	E	E				
Searching via Computer					I	I	R	E	E				
Primary/Secondary Sources					I	I	I	R	R	E			
Using Equipment		I	I	R	R	R	E	E	R	E		E	

[Handwritten: Using Periodical Indexes → Access 3.2]

*[Handwritten: Primary/Secondary Sources * Key item! I.S.S. → 2.1 & 2.2]*

[Handwritten: I.U. 4.1]

	K	1	2	3	4	5	6	7	8	9	10	11	12
Research Skills													
Selecting a Topic						I	I	E	E	E	E	E	
Using Appropriate Sources						I	I	R	E	E	E	E	
Taking Notes						I	I	R	R	E	E	E	
Footnotes							I	R	E	E	R	E	
Bibliography						I	R	R	E	E	R	E	

[Handwritten: 1.1 Selecting a Topic — TASK DEF.]
*[Handwritten: 2.1 & 2.2 Using Appropriate Sources * key item for I.S.S.]*
[Handwritten: 4.2 Taking Notes — I.U.]
[Handwritten: 4.2 Footnotes — I.U.]
[Handwritten: 4.2 Bibliography — I.U. & Synthesis 5.2]

NOTE: ASSUMES K-6 ELEMENTARY, 7-8 OR 7-9 MIDDLE, 9-12 OR 10-12 HIGH SCHOOL

*[Handwritten: → * The Research Process — key items]*

[handwritten heading across top:] Information Seeking Strategies: 2.1: det. range of sources.

[handwritten vertical label at left of table:] possible sources

	K	1	2	3	4	5	6	7	8	9	10	11	12
Types of Resources													
Information Books			I	I	R	E	E	E	E	R	E		
Indexes						I	I	E	E	E	E	E	
Dictionaries		I	I	R	R	R	R	R	E	R	R	E	R
Encyclopedias			I	I	R	R	E	E	R		E		
Atlases			I	I	R	R	E	E					
Almanacs					I	I	R	E	R	R	E		
Thesauri						I	I	I	R	R	E	E	
Vertical File		I	I	R	R	R	R	R	R	E	R		
Microform								I	R	R	E	E	
AV Software		I	I	R	R	R	R	E	E	R	E	R	
Computer Software		I	I	R	R	R	E	R	R	E	R		
Special Subject Sources													
Biographical Sources							I	I	I	R	R	E	E
Current Events Sources							I	I	I	R	R	E	E
Literary Sources							I	I	R	R	E	E	E
Arts Sources									I	R	E	E	E
Career Sources								I	R	R	E	E	E
Literature Appreciation													
Folk Tales	I	I	R	R	R	R	R	E	E	E	E		
Picture Books	I	R	R										
Poetry	I	I	R	R	R			E	E	E	E	E	E
Plays						I	I	R	E	R	R	E	E
Mythology	I	I	R	R	R	R	E	E	E	E	E	E	
Biography				I	R	R	E	R	R	E	R	R	
Fiction			I	I	R	E	E	E	R	R	E	E	
Literary Criticism								I	R	R	E	E	E

[handwritten box:] MISSING: human sources!

[handwritten note at lower left, arrow to Literature Appreciation:] Also part of the information services program.

[handwritten note at lower right:] a little in TASK Definition, Mostly information seeking strategies. (Could also be info. use)

I = INSTRUCT, R=REVIEW/REINFORCE, E = EXPAND

[handwritten notes at bottom:]

Notes: ① Coordinate Lit. App. with the language arts curriculum.
② Missing → evaluation. Need eval. of product + process.
③ Expand on TASK DEF., SYNTHESIS, EVAL.

Figure 4.4: Draft of Revised Library & Information Skills Curriculum

	K	1	2	3	4	5	6	7	8	9	10	11	12
TASK DEFINITION													
1.1 Define the Problem													
Selecting a Topic							I	I	E	E	E	E	E
Literature Appreciation													
1.2 Identify Information Requirements													
INFORMATION SEEKING STRATEGIES													
2.1 Determine Range of Sources													
Public Library			I	I	R	R	R	E	E	E	E	R	R
Academic Libraries										I	E	E	E
Primary/Secondary Sources						I	I	I	R	R	E	E	
Types of Resources													
Information Books			I	I	R	E	E	E	E	R	E		
Indexes						I	I	E	E	E	E	E	
Dictionaries		I	I	R	R	R	R	E	R	R	E	R	
Encyclopedias			I	I	R	R	E	E	R		E		
Atlases			I	I	R	R	E	E					
Almanacs					I	I	R	E	R	R	E		
Thesauri						I	I	I	R	R	E	E	
Vertical File		I	I	R	R	R	R	E	R	R	E	R	
Microform								I	R	R	E	E	
AV Software		I	I	R	R	R	R	E	E	R	E	R	
Computer Software			I	I	R	R	R	E	R	R	E	R	
Special Subject Sources													
Biographical Sources						I	I	I	R	R	E	E	
Current Events Sources						I	I	I	R	R	E	E	
Literary Sources							I	I	R	R	E	E	E
Arts Sources									I	R	E	E	E
Career Sources								I	R	R	E	E	E
Literature Appreciation													
Folk Tales	I	I	R	R	R	R	R	E	E	E	E		
Picture Books	I	R	R										
Poetry	I	I	R	R	R			E	E	E	E	E	E
Plays					I	I	R	E	R	R	E	E	E
Mythology	I	I	R	R	R	R	R	E	E	E	E	E	E
Biography				I	R	R	E	R	R	E	R	R	
Fiction				I	I	R	E	E	E	R	R	E	E
Literary Criticism								I	R	R	E	E	E
2.2 Determine Priorities													
Using Appropriate Sources							I	I	R	E	E	E	E
Primary/Secondary Sources						I	I	I	R	R	E	E	
Public Library			I	I	R	R	R	E	E	E	E	R	R
Academic Libraries										I	E	E	E

GAP ⟷ Requirements / Assignments

move elsewhere?

too much?

Too much?

GAP: Human Sources — interview, tv, radio, telephone

NOTE: ASSUMES K-6 ELEMENTARY, 7-8 OR 7-9 MIDDLE, 9-12 OR 10-12 HIGH SCHOOL

	K	1	2	3	4	5	6	7	8	9	10	11	12
LOCATION AND ACCESS													
3.1 Locate Physically and Intellectually													
Layout of the LMC	I	I	I	R	R	R	R	E	E	E	E		
Shelf Arrangement	I	I	I	R	R	R	R	E	E	E	E		
Reference Section			I	I	R	R	R	E	E	E	E	E	E
Nonfiction			I	I	R	R	E	E	E	E			
Fiction		I	I	R	R	R	E	E	E	E			
Biography			I	I	R	R	E	E	E	E			
Periodicals	I	I	R	R	R	R	E	E		E	E		R
AV materials	I	I	R	R	R	R	E	E		E	E		R
Equipment	I	I	R	R	R	R	E	E	E	E	E		R
Computers		I	I	R	R	R	E	E	E	E	E	E	
3.2 Find within Sources													
Catalog			I	I	R	R	R	E	E	E			
Dewey Decimal System			I	I	R	R	R	E	E	E			
Subject Headings			I	I	R	R	R	E	E	E			
Parts of a Book	I	I	R	R	R	E	E	E		E			
Using Back-of-the-Book Indexes			I	I	R	R	E			E			
Using Periodical Indexes						I	I	E	E	R	E	E	
Searching via Computer								I	I	R	E	E	E
INFORMATION USE													
4.1 Engage Information in a Source													
Using Equipment				I	I	R	R	R	E	E	R	E	E
4.2 Extract Information from a Source													
Circulation	I	I	I	R	R	R	R	E	E	E	E	R	R
Use Areas	I	I	I	R	R	R	R	E	E	E	E	R	R
Taking Notes							I	I	R	R	E	E	E
Footnotes								I	R	E	E	R	E
Bibliography							I	R	R	E	E	R	E
SYNTHESIS													
5.1 Organize from Multiple Sources													
5.2 Present Information													
Bibliography							I	R	R	E	E	R	E
EVALUATION													
6.1 Judge the Product													
6.2 Judge the Process													

Handwritten annotations:
- (brace beside Layout of the LMC through Equipment) *"Too much?"*
- (beneath 4.1 Engage Information in a Source) *"Using computers? GAP → listening || viewing || skimming"*
- (brace beside Taking Notes, Footnotes, Bibliography) *"citing?"*
- *"→ interviewing"*
- (beneath 5.1) *"GAP → organize = outlining"*
- (beside 5.2 Bibliography) *"GAP → Presentation formats / Graphics"*
- (beneath 6.1) *"GAP → product"*
- (beneath 6.2) *"GAP → process"*

I = INSTRUCT, R=REVIEW/REINFORCE, E = EXPAND

Figure 4.5: Revised Library & Information Skills Curriculum

	K	1	2	3	4	5	6	7	8	9	10	11	12
TASK DEFINITION													
1.1 Define the Problem													
Information Problems			I	I	R	R	R	E	E	R	E	R	R
Information Needs				I	I	R	R	R	R	E	R	R	
Selecting a Topic					I	I	R	R	E	E	E	E	E
Literature Appreciation	I	I	R	R	R	R	R	E	R	R	E	R	
1.2 Identify Information Requirements													
Analyzing Assignments			I	I	I	R	R	R	E	E	E	R	R
The Big Six Skills	I	I	R	R	R	R	R	E	E	R	E	R	R
INFORMATION SEEKING STRATEGIES													
2.1 Determine Range of Sources													
Types of Resources													
Categories - Text/Human	I	I	I	I	R	R	R	E	E	E	E	E	E
Brainstorming	I	I	I	I	R	R	R	E	E	E	E	E	E
Primary/Secondary Sources						I	I	I	R	R	E	E	
Text Resources													
Information (NF) Books			I	I	R	E	E	E	E	R	E		
Dictionaries		I	I	R	R	R	R	E	R	R	E	R	
Encyclopedias			I	I	R	R	E	E	R		E		
Indexes						I	I	E	E	E	E	E	
Other Reference Sources			I	I	R	R	E	E					
Resource File		I	I	R	R	R	R	E	R	R	E	R	
Periodicals								I	R	R	E	E	
Media		I	I	R	R	R	R	E	E	R	E	R	
Computer Software			I	I	R	R	E	E	R	R	E	R	
Special Subject Sources						I	I	I	R	R	E	E	
Literature	I	I	R	R	R	R	R	E	E	E	E	E	E
Literary Criticism								I	R	R	E	E	E
External Sources													
Telephone			I	I	R	R	E	E		E	E		
Public Library			I	I	R	R	R	E	E	E	E	R	R
Academic Libraries										I	E	E	E
Human Resources													
Interview			I	I	R	R	R	E	E	E	E	R	R
Television	I	I	R	R	R	R	R	E	E	E	E		
Radio						I	I	I	I	R	R	E	E
Speech/Presentation				I	I	I	R	R	R	R	R	E	E
2.2 Determine Priorities													
Using Appropriate Sources	I	I	I	I	R	R	R	E	E	R	E	E	E
Decision-Making	I	I	R	R	R	E	E	R	R	R	E		
Primary/Secondary Sources						I	I	I	R	R	E	E	
Public Library			I	I	R	R	R	E	E	E	E	R	R
Academic Libraries										I	E	E	E
LOCATION AND ACCESS													
3.1 Locate Physically and Intellectually													
Layout/Arrangement	I	I	I	R	R	R	R	E	E	E	E		
Reference Section				I	I	R	R	R	E	E	E	E	E
Periodicals			I	I	R	R	R	R	E	E		E	R
Media			I	I	R	R	R	R	E	E	E	E	R
Equipment			I	I	R	R	R	R	E	E	E	E	R
Computers			I	I	R	R	R	E	E	E	E	E	E

	K	1	2	3	4	5	6	7	8	9	10	11	12
3.2 Find within Sources													
Catalog			I	I	R	R	R	E	E	E	E		
Subject Headings/DDC			I	I	R	R	R	E	E	E	E		
Parts of a Book		I	I	R	R	R	E	E	E			E	
Using Back-of-the-Book Indexes			I	I	R	R	R	E				E	
Using Periodical Indexes						I	I	E	E	R	E	E	
Searching via Computer								I	I	R	E	E	E
INFORMATION USE													
4.1 Engage Information in a Source													
Using Equipment			I	I	R	R	R	E	E	R	E		E
Skimming			I	I	R	R	R	E	E	E			
Listening	I	I	R	R	R	E	E	R	R	R	E	E	
Viewing	I	I	R	R	R	E	E	R	R	R	E	E	
Using Computers (Full-Text)				I	I	I	R	R	R	R	E	E	E
Literature Appreciation													
Folk Tales	I	I	R	R	R	R	R	E	E	E	E		
Picture Books	I	R	R										
Poetry	I	I	R	R				E	E	E	E	E	E
Plays					I	I	R	E	R	R	E	E	E
Mythology	I	I	R	R	R	R	R	E	E	E	E	E	E
Biography				I	R	R	E	R	R	E	R	R	
Fiction				I	I	R	E	E	E	R	R	E	E
4.2 Extract Information from a Source													
Circulation	I	I	I	R	R	R	R	E	E	E	E	R	R
Use Areas	I	I	I	R	R	R	R	E	E	E	E	R	R
Taking Notes		I	I	I	R	R	R	E	E	R	R	E	E
Citing		I	I	I	R	R	R	E	E	R	R	E	E
Footnotes/Bibliography		I	I	I	R	R	R	E	E	R	R	E	E
Interviewing			I	I	R	R	R	E	E	R	R	E	
SYNTHESIS													
5.1 Organize from Multiple Sources													
Methods (e.g. Using Notecards)				I	I	I	R	R	R	E	E	E	
Writing with a Computer				I	I	I	R	R	R	E	E	E	
Outlining				I	I	I	R	R	R	E	E	E	
5.2 Present Information													
Choosing a format				I	I	I	R	R	R	E	E	E	
Essay					I	I	R	E	R	R	E	R	R
Report				I	I	R	E	R	R	R	E	R	R
Speech						I	I	R	R	E	R	E	E
Video							I	I	I	R	R	E	E
Graphics	I	I	R	R	E	E	E	R	R	R	E	E	
Graphing					I	I	R	R	R	E	E	E	
Bibliography							I	R	R	E	E	R	E
EVALUATION													
6.1 Judge the Product													
Setting Criteria			I	I	R	R	R	E	R	R	E	R	E
Comparisons			I	I	R	R	R	R	R	R	E	R	E
Making/Completing Checklists								I	I	R	R	E	E
6.2 Judge the Process													
Big Six Skills	I	I	R	R	R	E	R	R	E	E	E	E	E
Diary/Journal					I	I			I	R	E	E	
Styles Assessment				I	I	R	R	R	E	E	E		

Curriculum is the conceptual heart of the educational process. Curriculum translates educational goals into learning experiences, and describes the specific interactions of students, teachers and subject matter. Any effort to teach library & information skills must be integrally involved with classroom content.

Beyond the practical value of teaching library & information skills in a classroom context, development of these skills is important for the attainment of classroom curriculum objectives. Competence in information problem-solving will greatly enhance a student's ability to learn content and fulfill the requirements of assignments. Teachers are supportive and enthusiastic when they see how library & information skills instruction directly relates to their own efforts.

Before library media specialists can integrate instructional efforts with classroom curriculum, they must know what the classroom curriculum is. Three techniques for collecting information on curriculum are offered below.

Collect assignments

Assignments represent an untapped "gold mine" of information about curriculum. Irving (1985) defines an assignment as *"any* task set for pupils by teachers which is designed to increase or enhance learning." (p. 26) Assignments* point to the most valued aspects of curriculum. By giving an assignment related to a particular area of curriculum, teachers are stating that area is important. Assignments also state what students are required to do, and how students are to expend most of their efforts.

Assignments are easy to consider from an information problem-solving perspective. Students are required to complete some task that almost always requires some information gathering and use. Fulfilling the assignment means that the students will synthesize (organize and present) the information. Lastly, before turning in the assignment, students are likely to consider whether they have successfully completed the task.

Irving (1985) promotes the development of study and information skills by "working through assignments" (p. 32). "Assignments, because they are what everyone *does,* are the most appropriate bases for discussing the planning and implementation of study skills" (p. 121). She identifies a nine step process for completing assignments that is similar in focus and scope to the Big Six Skills approach. Thus, one easy way to insure that library & information skills instruction is integrated with classroom curriculum is to tie the instructional effort to assignments.

---

*   Because tests and quizzes require students to do something, namely study and complete some form of assessment, they can be included in the assignments category.

Most library media specialists already collect some information about assignments from teachers. We suggest establishing an *Assignments File* organized by grade and teacher. Teachers should be informed of why the assignments are being collected and how they will be used. Systematic collection from teachers can take place through periodic notices, direct contact, and reminders at meetings. Other useful methods for acquiring assignments include:

- setting up an *Assignments Box* near the copy machine

- alerting faculty secretaries, aides, and clerks to make an extra copy of every assignment

- photocopying assignments from students when they ask for help in the library media center

- reviewing curriculum projects and locally developed curricula

- working with faculty through team, subject area, or grade level meetings.

Examine current efforts

It is also important to build on the existing instructional strengths of the library media program. Therefore, another important source for analysis and planning are the current efforts to teach library & information skills. Some efforts may be independent library & information skills units, others may already be integrated with specific classroom curriculum. In order to *rethink* current efforts from a Big Six Skills perspective, it is necessary to collect a range of data on:

- goals and objectives of the unit

- activities and exercises

- associated library & information skills (as currently defined)

- variables of instruction (including time frame, level of instruction, teaching methods, materials, evaluation method)

- assignments.

Figure 4.6 is a form designed to facilitate data gathering. Assignments and relevant worksheets can be attached to this form. The form also asks for a brief, initial assessment in relation to the Big Six Skills. Ultimately, each unit must be examined to determine necessary revisions and adaptations, and the placement of units within the overall instructional plan.

The Library & Information Skills Instructional Program:
Review of Existing Integrated Unit

Curriculum Information:

Unit Name: _____
Teacher: _____
Grade: _____
Calendar Quarter: _____
Total Time: _____

Brief Description of the Content
(subject matter covered):

General Description of the Unit
(activities and sequence):

Library Media Program Information:

Library Media Services:

Information Service: _____
_____
_____

Reading Guidance Service: _____
_____
_____

Consultation Service: _____
_____
_____

Resources:	Uses (describe):
☐ nonfiction	_____
☐ fiction	_____
☐ reference	_____
☐ periodical	_____
☐ media	_____
☐ computer	_____
☐ human	_____
☐ other	_____

Current Library & Information
Skills Focus:

Relationship to the Big Six Skills:

	Direct	Indirect	Unclear	Note
Task Definition	☐	☐	☐	_____
Info. Seek. Strat.	☐	☐	☐	_____
Location & Access	☐	☐	☐	_____
Use of Information	☐	☐	☐	_____
Synthesis	☐	☐	☐	_____
Evaluation	☐	☐	☐	_____

Figure 4.6: Worksheet for Review of Existing Integrated Unit

Curriculum mapping

Curriculum mapping is a systematic process to collect, organize and present information on the "real" curriculum of the school. Curriculum information as presented in curriculum guides and syllabi represent what the writers *hope* the curriculum will be, not what the curriculum really is. English (1978) refers to this type of curriculum information as "fiction." Therefore, curriculum guides are of limited value for the library media program concerned with identifying key areas for integration with skill instruction and developing of specific information problem-solving learning activities.

The curriculum mapping process involves:

(1) Collecting data on actual curriculum units

(2) Organizing the data by fields of interest (e.g., subject area, time period, grade)

(3) Presenting the data in some form of table or chart.

The completed chart is a curriculum map. The map can then be examined to identify promising units for integrated Big Six Skills instruction. Of course, the maps are useful for a range of other needs as well (e.g., determining areas of need for services provision and collection building).

Curriculum mapping has been widely accepted and applied by library media specialists. A few have criticized the approach as being too time-consuming to implement. This is completely false.

The curriculum mapping process does not require an inordinate amount of time. It is not necessary to map every curriculum unit in a school or district. Some options include:

• collecting only one or two significant units per teacher

• surveying one or two entire grade levels or subject areas

• making initial contacts with previously cooperative teachers.

The objective is to gather information about a reasonable number of significant units in the curriculum. For example, if each teacher in a school with 45 teachers provides information on two or three units, the library media specialist will have over 100 units to consider for possible integration. Information about additional units can be solicited and added to the curriculum map at a later time.

In terms of the data collection, it takes most teachers less than five minutes to complete one curriculum mapping worksheet (see figure 4.7). The worksheet documents over eleven variables about a unit. Organizing data and creating a map are straightforward tasks that are easily accomplished with a simple file management program on any type of computer. See Appendix B for sample curriculum maps and *Curriculum Initiative* for more information on the mapping process.

The bottom line is that curriculum mapping *saves time* by providing, in a direct and concise manner, the information about curriculum required to plan the program. It's time-consuming to find out about classroom curriculum in an informal, haphazard manner. It's time-consuming to attempt to plan for integrated instruction without reliable information about the curriculum.

DEVELOP AND DOCUMENT PLANS FOR THE INTEGRATED LIBRARY & INFORMATION SKILLS PROGRAM

Planning for integrated skills instruction takes place on two levels: (1) an overview of general intentions over time, and (2) specific unit and lesson plans. Additional tools for planning on these levels are offered below and in chapters 5 and 6.

Creating a timeline

A number of planning tools and formats that document the general plan are offered in *Resource Companion to Curriculum Initiative* including the *skills by unit* matrix and the yearly *schedule of units* (see section I.3 of *Resource Companion*). A number of library media specialists have written or commented that they like to use a combination of the two – a general timeline with a place to note emphasis in terms of Big Six Skills. This was presented as figure 7.6 in *Curriculum Initiative* and is reproduced in a revised format here as figure 4.8. This planning format provides a concise explanation of the intentions over the year. It is also easy to scan the chart in order to identify potential scheduling bottlenecks or gaps in Big Six Skills instruction.

Developing generic lessons

Formal planning on the strategic level involves developing unit and lesson plans. Formats for unit and lesson plans are available in *Resource Companion to Curriculum Initiative*, and exemplary units are presented in the next chapter.

In addition, in implementing a Big Six Skills approach, a number of people have found it useful to develop short *generic lessons* that can be used in conjunction with almost any subject area instructional endeavor. A generic lesson is a planned instructional effort that focuses on one aspect of the Big Six Skills approach. This

Curriculum Mapping Data Collection Worksheet

School

Grade: _____   Date: _____

Teacher: _____   Number of Sections: ____

Number of Students: ____

Subject: _____   Course: _____

Unit: _____

Total Periods of Instruction: _____

Calendar Quarter: _____

Level of Instruction:
____ introduced
____ reinforced
____ expanded
comment: _____
_____

Materials:
____ text
____ one source
____ multiple sources
comment: _____
_____

Organization of Instruction:
____ large group
____ small group
____ individual

comment: _____
_____

Primary Teaching Method:
____ desk work
____ lecture
____ demonstration
____ discussion
____ independent study
____ programmed
(includes learning stations)
____ project
____ report
comment: _____
_____

Evaluation:
____ test
____ observation
____ short written assignment
____ product
____ report
____ project
comment: _____
_____

Note: This is a sample worksheet that should be customized to meet the needs of your own situation.

Figure 4.7: Curriculum Mapping Worksheet

Figure 4.8: Elementary School Schedule with Big Six Skills Noted

Week in the School Year																				Big Six Skills to emphasize						Comments
Subject	2	4	6	8	10	12	14	16	18	20	22	24	26	28	30	32	34	36	38	40	TD	IS	LA	UI	SY	EV	Comments
KINDERG.																											
Lang. Arts																											
Math				------NUMBERS------																1	2		4			major unit
Reading					............letter-sounds............																	3				year long
Science																											
Soc. Studies																											
GRADE 1																											
Lang. Arts			----------------LITERATURE-------------																	1		3		5		major unit
Math																											
Reading																											
Science		animals																			1	2					booktalk
Soc. Studies									FAMILIES				map skills								1			4	5	6	major unit
GRADE 2																											
Lang. Arts	............listening skills............																					2		4			audio tapes
Math																											
Reading																											
Science														SOLAR SYSTEM							1		3	4			major unit
Soc. Studies								neighborhoods																	5		
GRADE 3																											
Lang. Arts																											
Math																											
Reading							ORDER of EVENTS																		5	6	
Science											food groups																
Soc. Studies											COMM RESOURCES										1	2	3		5		great unit
GRADE 4																											grade 4 needs
Lang. Arts																											more develop.
Math																											
Reading	...dictionary skills...																										1st unit
Science																											
Soc. Studies														COL/REV							1	2	3		5	6	major unit
GRADE 5																											good year
Lang. Arts														BIOGRAPHY								2			5	6	major unit
Math						graphs																		4			
Reading																											
Science			ANIMALS																		1				5	6	expand gr1
Soc. Studies			immigration																			2	3				
GRADE 6																											
Lang. Arts				MYTHS				...vocabulary (year long)...														2			5	6	major unit
Math																											
Reading				............main idea............																				4			
Science													electricity														
Soc. Studies			map skills																					4	5		

Key:

TD	=	Task Definition	UI =	Use of Information
IS	=	Info. Seek. Strategy	SY =	Synthesis
LA	=	Location & Access	EV =	Evaluation

one aspect may relate to any of the three levels (the broad information problem-solving process, the Big Six Skills, or specific components of the Big Six Skills).

The key to using generic lessons is the phrase *in conjunction with*. Generic lessons are only valuable if tied to a curriculum unit or lesson. Attempting to deliver a generic lesson independent of any curriculum would be a step backwards to the days of teaching isolated library skills removed from any classroom context.

Chapter 6 provides a number of generic lessons that can be easily adapted to local situations. Lesson number 2, for example, focuses on helping students to work through information seeking strategies. A checklist is provided that can be revised to cover potential resources in the local environment. Since it is reasonable to focus on information seeking strategies whenever students are faced with an assignment that requires a range of resources, this generic unit can be applied to a number of different subject areas. The time frame for delivering the lesson is also flexible: the library media specialist could (a) use the checklist to quickly introduce information seeking strategies, or (b) review the checklist after an extensive discussion of options and priorities. There are other possibilities as well. The main value of the generic lesson is that it provides an initial structure to assist the library media specialist in delivering the desired instruction.

The generic lessons in chapter 6 can be considered as the initial entries in a master file of generic lessons. As library media specialists plan and deliver integrated Big Six Skills instruction, they are likely to develop a range of supporting instructional tools, means, and methods. These various techniques are applicable in other situations as well. By documenting successful lessons in a file of generic lessons, library media specialists can build up an invaluable resource for planning and teaching.

CONCLUSION

This chapter has offered a number of different actions to facilitate implementing a library & information skills instructional program based on information problem-solving. These or similar actions, are necessary to:

- establish the library & information skills objectives

- analyze the school curriculum

- develop overall and specific plans for instruction.

The remainder of this book is devoted to providing examples of successful library and information skills instructional efforts that are based on the Big Six Skills and integrally tied to subject area curricula.

Chapter 5
Exemplary Library & Information Skills Instructional Units

At this point, you are familiar with the philosophy behind the Big Six Skills approach, and the general concepts that implement it. One of the basic assumptions is that educational goals are attainable when the methodology is well-designed and organized. Another basic assumption is that school library media specialists and teachers who engage in a collaborative process of instructional design and development are working to ensure that students are engaged in purposeful activities.

The unit plans presented here are based on collaboratively designed instructional units that were submitted by practicing school library media specialists from across the United States. Although each contributing library media specialist was asked to use the same Unit Design Format, (based on *Curriculum Initiative* and *Resource Companion to Curriculum Initiative*), each person changed the original design to accommodate individual needs. This practice is certainly appropriate and desirable. Some library media specialists prefer detailed plans, others find them to be restrictive. The style of the document is less important than the quality of instruction that results from careful planning.

Through creativity and adaptability it is possible to modify these units to suit local goals. It is also appropriate to use them as a reference for the design of instructional units. Individuality, the resources available in a school library media center, and the climate of cooperation between the library media specialist and teachers can act as standards by which to personalize these units to local situations. In the end, it is hoped that these exemplary units will serve as additions to, or models for the continued development of a school's integrated library & information skills instructional program.

The Wonderful World of Birds

Shan Glandon,
Jenks West
Elementary
School,
Jenks, OK
74037

Shan Glandon, library media specialist from Jenks West Elementary School (Jenks, OK) sent us a multi-faceted instructional unit taught at the primary school level (Grade 2 - Science). After reviewing this plan, it is easy to understand why students are easily motivated from beginning to end. Dividing the instruction into multiple parts, mini-topics, and high-interest activities, allows students to put together a complete nature study about birds. The concentration on the Big Six Skills of task definition, location and access, use of information and synthesis provides students with the information problem-solving structure necessary for success. – ME/RB

Unit Summary

Audience: 2nd Grade (Science)

Overview:
This project is designed to provide opportunities for students to:
1.   explore the world of birds, their habitat and habits
2.   discover the variety of materials about birds available in the library
3.   read, view, listen, think about and communicate information accurately and effectively.

Rationale:
The 2nd grade science text offers units on animals of long ago and their descendants. The classroom teachers were interested in a more in-depth study of one group of animals. This bird unit was planned as a follow-up to previous text-based science units.

Subject Area Objectives:
1.   Develop an awareness of the process of scientific study: observe, gather, record information, and hypothesize.
2.   Describe and identify the properties of living things.
3.   Become aware of the adaptations animals make to survive.
4.   Demonstrate care and respect for living things.

Big Six Skills Objectives:
1.   **Task Definition**
      Identifies key words in a question.
3.   **Location and Access**
      Uses the card catalog (with assistance) and spine labels to locate materials on the shelf.
      Locates encyclopedias.
      Uses guide words to locate a topic in an encyclopedia.
      Uses index and table of contents.
4.   **Use of Information**
      Summarizes information from a source.
5.   **Synthesis**
      Conveys information accurately in written sentences.
      Uses illustrations and charts to present information.

Unit Organization

Preparation Activities:
1.   The library media specialist and teacher create a bulletin board for the classroom, titled "The Wonderful World of Birds." The teacher prepares a tree and the letters and the library media provides bird shapes with an assignment pasted on the back of each bird. The assignments are based on resources available in the library.

2.   The library media specialist prepares a bibliography of resources on birds.

3.   The teacher contacts the Cooperative Extension Service to arrange for an incubator and eggs for hatching.

4.   The library media specialist makes transparencies illustrating the structure of feathers, the different kinds of feathers - wings, body, down, and tail; bird feet and tracks; and bird beaks.

5.   The library media specialist chooses a story about birds to read aloud.

6.   The teacher makes a chart illustrating simple tools: tweezers, nutcrackers, hammers, probes, strainers, knives and drills.

Activities and Materials

Activities:

Day 1 Activities:
1. "What is a bird?" The teacher writes this question on the board and begins a discussion with students. All ideas are listed. Students watch a video on birds to identify bird characteristics. Follow-up discussion narrows and focuses students' definitions.

2. The teacher refers back to previous study of dinosaurs to recall information about early birds, then assigns a small group of students to research and make charts about Archaeopteryx and Pterosaurs. Charts include information and illustrations.

3. Teacher begins reading groups. For this unit the Basal Reader is set aside and three books by Bill Peet were chosen as readers. All three have birds as the main character.

Day 2 Activities:
1. In story hour the library media specialist shares Animal Fact/Animal Fable by Seymour Simon. Each student chooses a bird from the bulletin board for his/her research. The bird picture identifies the resource to be used and the fact/fable that needs to be researched.

2. Using the transparencies, the teacher begins instruction and discussion on bird feathers. Encourage students to look for feathers and bring them to the classroom. Tape each feather to chart paper and identify the bird to which it belonged. Some questions to include: Why are male birds often brightly colored and females rather dull in color? Are there any birds where the opposite is true? Words to identify and discuss include *preening*, *molting* and *plumage*.

Day 3 Activities:
1. The library media specialist works with the group as a whole to review the Big Six Skills.

2. Students are divided into small groups to define their tasks and identify the search strategy that can be used to help develop a chart to identify birds by the color of their feathers.

3. Reading groups continue.

Day 4 Activities:
1. Reading groups continue.

2. Fact/fable research begins. Students work in small groups with the library media specialist. Instruction is given on using call numbers to locate materials on the shelf. Students locate their materials and begin to read.

3. Teacher uses the transparencies to start instruction and discussion on bird feet and tracks.

Days 5, 6, & 7 Activities:
1. Reading groups continue.

2. Fact/fable research continues.

3. The teacher begins instruction and discussion of bird beaks and their uses. Show video, "Bird Beaks and Behavior"(Many Worlds of Nature, Morse-Allen Productions, OETA, Oklahoma Department of Education.).

4. Students draw colorful pictures of birds without their beaks. They then select any tool from the chart of tools and draw it as the beak for their bird. Students write a short explanation of how the bird uses its new beak.

5. Brainstorm a list of what birds eat. Additional activity is to have students build bird feeders, hang the bird feeders outside the classroom windows and conduct experiments, recording data in notebooks.

6. The teacher conducts a discussion on the energy needs of birds. Birds burn up a lot of energy: many baby birds and adults eat twice their weight in food each day. Have students figure out how many pounds of food they would have to eat in a day to eat like a baby bird.

Day 8 Activities:
1. Reading groups continue.

2. Fact/fable research continues.

3. Begin discussion and instruction on where birds live. Discuss types of habitats, and characteristics of each bird. Have students work in pairs and create three-dimensional habitat miniatures using shoe boxes. Add drawings of birds to the miniature habitat.

4. Begin discussion and instruction on bird nests. As an experiment, take a trip outside and place short lengths of yarn and string (5 - 10 inches long) in grassy

and bushy areas for birds to pick up. Check daily and keep a log.

Days 9 & 10 Activities:
1. Reading groups finish.

2. Fact/fable research finishes.

3. Begin discussion (use appropriate AV software as available) on the life cycle of a bird. Introduce incubator and egg-hatching project.

4. Play a recording of bird sounds and engage students in a discussion about birds and their songs.

5. Check the incubator.

Day 11 Activities:
1. Talk about the concepts *endangered* and *extinct*. Have students, working in pairs, design a poster that will interest people in protecting an endangered bird.

2. Check the incubator.

Day 12 Activities:
1. Go on a bird-watching expedition. Invite a local bird enthusiast to lead students on the nature walk (contact Audubon Society or local nature center for assistance).

2. Check the incubator.

Day 13 Activities:
1. The library media specialist reads the student research reports on bird facts/ fables to the class. The reports are bound and made a permanent part of the library's collection.

2. Check the incubator. If eggs have not hatched by this day, keep checking until they do. Enjoy students' discovery when it happens!

Evaluation:
All products are reviewed by both the library media specialist and classroom teacher for accuracy, clarity, and completeness.

Basic Resources:

"Birds," *Animals and How They Grow*. National Geographic Society, 1976.

Birds. (Video) National Geographic Society, 1978, 12 minutes, color.

Burnie, David. *Bird*. Alfred A. Knopf (Eyewitness Books), 1988.

Peet, Bill. *Fly Homer Fly*. Houghton Mifflin, 1969.

Peet, Bill. *The Pinkish, Purplish, Bluish Egg*. Houghton Mifflin, 1963.

Peet, Bill. *The Spooky Tail of Prewitt Peacock*. Houghton Mifflin, 1973.

Fact or Fable Research List:
1) Eagles have excellent eyesight.
2) Birds have several kinds of feathers.
3) Birds have bones like human beings.
4) "Like water off a duck's back" means birds are not bothered by anything.
5) Birds and reptiles molt.
6) Birds migrate because they do not like where they live.
7) If an animal has feathers, it must be a bird.
8) Penguins are birds.
9) The largest bird is the pelican.
10) The Downy Woodpecker's eating habits do not change with the seasons.
11) Pelicans carry things in their beaks.
12) Birds of prey eat live animals.
13) A grouse is a partridge.
14) The roadrunner, a desert bird, is a member of the cuckoo family.
15) Owls are wise old birds.
16) Baby geese will choose the first animal they see to be their mom or dad.
17) All birds fly.
18) All bird toes look alike.
19) Only birds have wings.
20) Birds have teeth.
21) The food a bird eats is determined by the kind of beak it has.
22) Hummingbirds fly like no other bird.
23) Birds build many kinds of nests.
24) Birds hatch from eggs.

Conclusion

From a Big Six Skills perspective, "The Wonderful World of Birds" provides primary school students an extended opportunity to use library & information problem-solving skills to learn about a topic that is both interesting and important to the science curriculum. Throughout the unit there are many opportunities for students to define tasks, develop strategies, and use and share information. One benefit the library media specialist has when integrating library & information skills into an instructional unit that lasts as long as this one is continuity. Continuity of instruction, in this instance, is based on focusing students' attention on one area of concern around which the Big Six Skills can be developed. There is sufficient time to teach the Big Six Skills, monitor how students apply them, and still review or remediate if necessary – all as part of the same instructional unit.
– ME/RB

Local History: History of the Erie Canal

**Lynn K. Morgan
Carthage Central
School,
Carthage, NY
13619**

Although this unit centers specifically on a topic of regional interest in New York State, Lynn Morgan, library media specialist in Carthage, NY, reminds us of the many opportunities that exist when library & information skills instruction is integrated with local history. In this 4th-grade unit, "Local History of the Erie Canal," the main Big Six Skills focus is on information seeking strategies and use of information. This is accomplished through review and reinforcement of skills. Lynn wrote that the strength of this unit was due to the cooperation among the classroom teacher, the music teacher and the library media specialist in its design, development and implementation.
– ME/RB

Unit Summary

Audience: Grade 4

Overview:
In cooperation with the classroom teacher and the music teacher, this three-week unit highlights the history and importance of the Erie Canal. Atlas and encyclopedia skills are taught so that students can effectively integrate these resources as part of their research strategy.

Rationale:
The fourth-grade social studies curriculum focuses on New York State and local history. The Erie Canal endures in the folklore, legends and music that it inspired. This unit emphasizes the tremendous impact of the canal on the growth of New York. From a library skills perspective, basic atlas and encyclopedia use skills will be taught to reinforce their importance within information seeking strategies.

Subject Area Objectives:
1. Students will be able to state the reasons the Erie Canal was constructed.
2. Students will be able to describe how the canal was built, by whom, the route, events during its building, how the canal was used, and life on the canal.
3. Students will be able to locate four major canals that make up the barge system.
4. Students will be able to explain the importance of the Barge Canal system to New York State.

Big Six Skills Objectives:
1. **Task Definition:** Students will brainstorm areas of interest, and create research questions based on topics.
2. **Information Seeking Strategies:** The importance of using atlases and encyclopedias as part of an information seeking strategy will be reinforced.
4. **Use of Information:** Use of atlases and encyclopedias will be reviewed. Students will take notes from reference books.
5. **Synthesis:** Student groups will decide how best to present to their classmates the information found. Students will present information.

Unit Organization

lesson	time frame	accountability	location	Big Six Skills
introduction	2 days	T	C	1
songs	2 days	music teacher	music	1
LMC intro.	2 days	LMS	LMC	1, 2
key words	1 day	LMS	LMC	2
topic selection	1 day	T/LMS	LMC	1, 2
bibliography	1 day	LMS/T	LMC	3
reference	3-4 days	student	LMC/C	3, 4, 5
presentation	2 days	student	C/LMC	5

Key:

	C	= Classroom
	T	= Teacher
	LMC	= Library Media Center
	LMS	= Library Media Specialist
Big Six Skills		= Library & Information Skills
	1	= task definition
	2	= information seeking strategies
	3	= location and access
	4	= use of information
	5	= synthesis
	6	= evaluation

Activities and Materials

Activities:

- focus on important information use skills using encyclopedias and atlases in small group activities

- create an Erie Canal Learning Center in the LMC

- help students decide on presentation modes

- present projects to classmates with opportunities to provide positive feedback

- provide debate and panel discussion opportunities for students to discuss the information they discovered about the Erie Canal.

Evaluation:
Joint teacher/LMS/student evaluation to identify strengths and weaknesses as well as areas for improvement of information seeking strategy, use and presentation.

Materials:
Atlases, encyclopedias, New York State maps, AV software as available, visuals

Follow-up/Supplemental Activities:
Field trip to the Erie Canal Village and/or Erie Canal Museum

Conclusion

From a Big Six Skills perspective, this unit requires students to consider ways to organize and present information. Alternative presentation forms, designed by the teacher and library media specialist, can be modeled for students within the learning center. Such models give students concrete examples by which to develop criteria for choosing appropriate methods to present information. Additionally, models give students benchmarks with which to gauge their personal strengths and weaknesses in presenting information.

"Local History of the Erie Canal" presents a unit that transcends the specifics of New York State. No matter where you are, regional history is a great topic on which to base an integrated library & information skills instructional unit. In submitting this unit, Lynn Morgan reminds us that an important byproduct of the integrated library & information skills instructional model is the understanding, involvement and ownership that results from communication. One successful unit leads to others, and that helps create a vigorous atmosphere for program growth. – ME/RB

Map-It

Joyce Richards
Prairie Grove
Elementary
School
Prairie Grove,
AR 72703

Joyce Richards, Media Specialist for the Prairie Grove Public Schools in Prairie Grove, AR, developed a unit that teaches students the skills they need to successfully integrate the use of atlases and maps into their information problem-solving strategy. The major focus of this 5-6th grade unit is on two of the Big Six Skills: Information Seeking Strategy and Synthesis. Although students prepare information for presentation, the opportunity to expand their resource choices through awareness, instruction, and use helps them to incorporate new reference tools into effective information problem-solving strategies. Joyce told us that students are able to present the information they find in various and interesting ways, such as: simple sketches of the school grounds, maps of the route from home to school, helium balloon launch with returns posted on a map, papier-mache globes, and maps of imaginary lands. Although Joyce teaches this unit in the upper elementary grades, it is certainly possible to adapt this unit for use in lower grades, as well as for junior high school students. ME/RB

Unit Summary

Audience: 5-6th grade

Overview:
In this unit, the Big Six Skills focus is on information seeking strategies. This unit introduces and reinforces map skills and terms through brainstorming and library resource-based activities. Each student will develop a vocabulary list related to the study of maps, and a bibliography of sources appropriate to learning about the study of maps. Additionally, students create projects, which will incorporate map terms and skills, and verify that the information seeking strategy was appropriate to the defined task.

Rationale:
This unit integrates Big Six Skills with the classroom content. The unit ends with a project to teach and reinforce map terms and skills. Students focus on the process of developing successful information seeking strategies through completing a project.

Objectives:
1. To introduce and reinforce map skills and terms.
2. To create a project that demonstrates students' level of ability with maps and map-related vocabulary.
3. To create a list of subject areas and topics that can be used as a master list for a resource search.
4. To design and conduct a LMC search that will produce appropriate resources for selected terms as defined.
5. To produce a map-oriented project for display at a Map-It Fair.

Big Six Skills Objectives:
Information Seeking Strategies:
Students will demonstrate the ability to prepare a vocabulary list related to the study of maps.

Students will demonstrate the ability to design an information seeking strategy for three selected terms.

Students will demonstrate the ability to prepare a selected bibliography of sources for three of the terms listed, giving the reason each source selected is important to the defined task.

Synthesis:
Each student will complete a project related to the study of maps using the sources from one of the bibliographies he/she developed.

Unit Organization, Activities and Materials

lesson	time frame	location	Big Six Skills
1.	45 min.	C	1

The classroom teacher introduces the unit of study and its requirements. Examples of student projects and project ideas are discussed. The teacher uses the textbook to introduce and review map skills and related terms. Students begin to generate a list of topics and terms.

2.	45 min.	LMC	1

The library media specialist uses av or computer software to review and reinforce basic map skills and terms. Each student compiles a vocabulary list related to the study of maps.

3.	45 min.	LMC	1, 2

The library media specialist reviews basic location and access tools appropriate to the study of maps. Students use tools to expand their vocabulary list. Students will isolate three main areas of interest and use them as topics to develop selective bibliographies on map study.

4.   3 - 5 days @ 60 min./day   LMC & C   2
Students will design an information seeking strategy, and prepare a bibliography for their 3 topics. Students annotate each item, answering such questions as: How did I come across this source? Why was or wasn't this source of information useful to meet the task? Did this source help me find other sources of information?

5.   3 weeks   LMC, C, &   5
                              Homework
Students will select one of the topics, pursue their research interest, and prepare a project to share with other students at the Map-It Fair. The library media specialist and teacher assist students in developing criteria for choosing an appropriate presentation format, selecting a project, and completing the project. (Presentation formats may vary: e.g., computer graphics, drawings, video, models, posters, games, storyboard, etc.)

6.   1 day   LMC   6
Students will display projects at the Map-It Fair. All students will be invited to the library media center to learn about maps from the projects presented by fellow students.

Key:

C	= Classroom
T	= Teacher
LMC	= Library Media Center
LMS	= Library Media Specialist
Big Six Skills	= Library & Information Skills
1	= task definition
2	= information seeking strategies
3	= location and access
4	= use of information
5	= synthesis
6	= evaluation

Evaluation:
Projects will be displayed at a Map-It Fair. Each student's work receives a recognition award. The annotated bibliography is reviewed to evaluate the student's information seeking strategy.

Materials:
AV or computer software to review map terms
art and craft materials

Follow-up/Supplemental Activities:

Design treasure map activities to provide a *fun* exercise for students.

Arrange for a surveyor, cartographer, or other map-related professional to visit the class.

Take a field trip with a surveyor to learn firsthand what a surveyor does and why it is important.

Have each student keep a research diary. The diary should include comments of how the search proceeded, successes, failures, approaches, etc. This diary can be reviewed by focusing on the Big Six Skill of Information Seeking Strategies.

Conclusion

When students work hard to prepare a project it is important that they be given an opportunity for sharing. "Map-It" is a good example of designing a unit rich in information skills instruction, which provides an atmosphere conducive for student recognition. Students get evaluative feedback on their project from fellow students as well as from the library media specialist and classroom teacher. From a Big Six Skills perspective, this evaluation provides an important opportunity to discuss the information problem-solving process in general, and an individual's information problem-solving style in particular. The Big Six Skills of information seeking strategies and synthesis can be enhanced through a final discussion of evaluation and its two component skills, effectiveness and efficiency. – ME/RB

Travel Brochures

Angela Ivanovic,
Library Media Specialist
Beth Pomerantz,
English Teacher
Mt. Lebanon Junior
High School
Pittsburgh,PA
15228

Diane Romm,
Library Media Specialist/
Department Chairperson
Christine Fiore,
Spanish Teacher
Uniondale School Dist.
Uniondale, NY
11553

Angela Ivanovic and Beth Pomerantz from Pitts-burgh, PA, teach the Big Six Skills in an integrated instructional unit they call "Travel Brochures." Special emphasis is placed on synthesis and the components organization and presentation of in-formation. A similar unit submitted by Diane Romm and Christine Fiore from Uniondale, NY, also contained good ideas and well-conceived library & information skills instructional strate-gies. Because of the high quality exemplified in both units, we decided to combine them into one. Taught as a coordinated effort, this unit can be integrated with the language arts, social studies, foreign language, and/or art curricula. Addition-ally, this unit can be easily adapted for use with a wide range of grade and ability levels. – ME/RB

Unit Summary

Audience: 7th Grade - English

Overview:
Students will create a travel brochure for a foreign country consisting of a cover depicting the area, information on climate, transportation, lodging, restaurants, and a specified number of tourist attractions.

Rationale:
The purpose of this unit is to incorporate research skills and descriptive and persuasive writing to produce a travel brochure.

Content Area Objectives:
Students will:
1.   organize information into a logical format for a travel brochure
2.   write concisely and persuasively about a prospective tour to an area
3.   employ correct usage, mechanics, and sentence construction in writing

4. incorporate information on climate, geography, transportation, and historic and other sites pertinent to a traveler
5. create an appealing cover to advertise a tour.

Major Big Six Skills Objectives:

Task Definition
Students will select a country and develop a travel brochure which would entice people to learn more about or visit the area.

Students will speculate as to what kinds of resources and how much research is required to successfully satisfy their information needs.

Information Seeking Strategies
Students will review and analyze travel brochures acquired from local travel agencies to help determine their information needs.

After selecting a country or region, students will read about it in a general encyclopedia and identify specific information needs sufficient to meet the requirements of the assignment.

A variety of reference sources will be reviewed with students. The students will then determine which are best to meet their specific information needs.

Students will prepare a simple research strategy consisting of a list of possible library resources that might be used to obtain information related to the assignment, a list of topics to be researched, and the method by which they will search for and record information.

Location and Access
Students will locate print and nonprint materials on the country by using the card catalog, *Readers' Guide to Periodical Literature*, and pamphlet file. Students will identify relevant information within each source by using the index, table of contents, and cross references.

Use of Information
Students will analyze the information found to determine its usefulness, take notes using the method devised as part of the strategy, and keep track of resources used in order to prepare a bibliography.

Synthesis
Students will organize the information accessed as required by the task.

Evaluation
Students will verify that all of the requirements of the assignment have been met though peer conferencing.

Unit Organization:

lesson	time frame	accountability	location	Big Six Skills
one	1 period	T& LMS	LMC	1, 2
two	3 periods	LMS	LMC	3, 4, 5
three	1 period	LMS	LMC	5
four	3 periods	T	C	5, 6
five	1 period	T	C	5

Key:

C	= Classroom
T	= Teacher
LMC	= Library Media Center
LMS	= Library Media Specialist
Big Six Skills	= Library & Information Skills
1	= task definition
2	= information seeking strategies
3	= location and access
4	= use of information
5	= synthesis
6	= evaluation

Planning Time:
2 periods - one before the unit begins and one during the instructional process to make any adjustments

Activities and Materials

Activities:
Lesson 1: Students will randomly choose a country or region to study. Students will analyze professionally designed travel brochures to determine the kinds of information included. They will make a list of potential topics for research. Students will read an encyclopedia article to develop a base of knowledge about their country. Each student will also develop an information seeking strategy to determine the additional sources that might be used to obtain information they will include in their final product.

Note: Students often decide to form *travel agencies* and develop a company logo and/or slogan. Also, students can be assigned to work together, and choose topics that are geographically related. When this happens, they need to develop a format to present their information so that all of their individual brochures look as if they have come from the same *company*.

Lesson 2: The classroom teacher reviews note-taking technique. Students find appropriate resources by using the card catalog, *Readers' Guide* and pamphlet file or even interviewing people who have traveled to the country. They select appropriate information from each; take notes (work is checked each day by the classroom teacher); and maintain a list of the sources used in the research process.

Lesson 3: Students continue their research. Students arrange the sources listed into a bibliography.

Lesson 4: Students organize their information by preparing a rough draft for each section of the final brochure. Generally students include such information as: map, flag, currency, food & drink, tourist attractions, pictures. Students revise and edit the rough draft of the brochure and participate in peer conferencing to determine if all the requirements of the assignment have been met.

Lesson 5: Students share the information about their country through a short oral presentation to the class.

Evaluation:
The research strategy, note-taking procedure, accuracy of information presented ·and final bibliography are evaluated by the library media specialist.

The classroom teacher evaluates the completed brochure and the oral presentation.

Materials:
Atlases
Almanacs
Encyclopedias
Readers' Guide to Periodical Literature
Reference Books
Pamphlet File
Assignment Sheet
Bibliography Style Sheet
Worksheet

Follow-up/Supplemental Activities:
Student work is displayed in the library media center, the English classroom, and in showcases throughout the building.

Students may write to various travel bureaus, chambers of commerce, and foreign tourist bureaus to obtain information related to their topic.

Students create an object or cook a food associated with their country. This can be included as part of their oral presentation.

The library media specialist can discuss letter writing as an information-gathering technique. After specific letter-writing instruction, students write letters to consulates requesting information about their country. (Brochures and other information received are contributed to the vertical file).

Conclusion

Units of study such as this one are easily adapted to meet a variety of needs. Students can study countries from which relatives immigrated, or countries participating in special sporting events. Whatever the content rationale might be, the information problem-solving process remains the same. Students design a strategy to meet an information need, and work through the process to be able to share and evaluate their final projects. From a Big Six Skills perspective, this is a major unit that can be used to introduce, review or extend students' competencies at library & information skills. Library resource-based instruction, combined with high interest content, provides the makings for enthusiastic learning.– ME/RB

Travel Brochure: Information Collection Worksheet*

Student: _____   Teacher: _____

Country: _____

Answer the following questions to help you gather the information you may want
to include in your travel brochure:

1.   How did your country get its name?

2.   Draw the flag of your country.

3.   What type of government does your country have and who is its current leader?

4.   Give the names of at least three famous people from your country and explain
     why they are famous.

5.   Name a national holiday and describe how it is observed.

6.   Name three places of interest to tourists and why they are special.

7.   What unit of currency is used in the country, and how much is it worth in
     American dollars?

8.   Draw a map of the country and label the capital, important cities, and important
     geographical features.

9.   Name and describe three foods that are eaten in the country.

10. How far is the capital of your country from New York City?

11. If you traveled to the country during July and August, what kind of clothes
     would you pack?

12. What is the international area code for your country?

_____

*   Diane Romm and Christine Fiore submitted this worksheet, which they use to help guide
students during their research process.

Words Worth Remembering

Nancy Rhead &
Alfreda Marino
Hammond Middle
School
Laurel, MD
20707

With its focus always pointed at the Big Six Skill of task definition, "Words Worth Remembering," an 8th-grade unit, also incorporates a strong evaluation element. As students work through each stage of the unit, they evaluate whether they are remaining on task. Designed by Alfreda Martino, library media specialist, and Nancy Rhead, reading teacher, at Hammond Middle School, Laurel, MD, this unit provides students with the opportunity to work individually and in small groups on research tasks. Alfreda and Nancy reminded us that this unit is also important because it gives students the opportunity to review their own philosophy and goals through the words of famous people. – ME/RB

Unit Summary

Audience: Grade 8 Reading - All Levels

Overview:
Each student will select, comprehend and research speeches or quotations that have had impact on life in America. Biographical, historical, and anecdotal information will be located and used in oral presentations that will explain the significance of the speech.

Rationale:
To be an effective reader, students must draw from a background of prior knowledge. Literary awareness is an important base for interpretive reading. Part of our store of knowledge is in our country's presidential inaugural speeches and other speeches and documents of historical importance.

Objectives:
1.   Students will read and comprehend speeches or quotations.
2.   Students will identify and use appropriate reference and library media center materials.
3.   Students will examine the historical context of the speech.
4.   Students will compare several speeches or quotations.
5.   Students will draw conclusions and make predictions from the speeches.
6.   Students will identify components of a well-written speech.
7.   Students will demonstrate oral presentation techniques.

Big Six Skills Objectives:

Task Definition
Students will understand the requirements of the assignment and be able to describe the requirements in their own words.

Information Seeking Strategies
Students will determine which reference sources to use to meet the defined task.

Location and Access
Students will compile the necessary information to meet the defined task.

Use of Information
Students will select the most appropriate information.

Synthesis
Students will organize, prepare and present an oral report.

Evaluation
Throughout the unit, students will check their activities to determine if they are keeping on task and following directions.

Unit Organization:

lesson	time frame	accountability	location	Big Six Skills
1.	3 periods	T	C	4
2.	1 period	T	LMC	4
3.	1 period	T	C	4
4.	2 periods	T	C	4
5.	2 periods	T & LMS	LMC	1,
6.	5 periods	LMS & T	LMC/PL	2, 3, 4
7.	2 weeks	S	homework	4, 5, 6
8.	1 week	S	C or LMC	5, 6

Key:

C	= Classroom
T	= Teacher
LMC	= Library Media Center
LMS	= Library Media Specialist
PL	= Public Library

Big Six Skills   = Library & Information Skills
         1   = task definition
         2   = information seeking strategies
         3   = location and access
         4   = use of information
         5   = synthesis
         6   = evaluation

Planning Time:
Two hours. The library media specialist assists the reading teacher in the selection and organization of sample speeches and quotations for students. (These selections can be compiled into individual notebooks for ease of student use.)

Activities and Materials

Activities:
1. Each student reads Dr. Martin Luther King, Jr.'s "I Have a Dream" speech. Students participate in a large group discussion about Dr. King's life and the historical context of the speech. Students carefully read and examine the speech to identify those components which make the speech effective and well- written. Students additionally identify uses of figurative language, and literary and historical references.

2. Students view a video of Dr. King's speech and discuss oral presentation techniques and Dr. King's presentation style.

3. Using the notebook of collected speeches, students will read or watch a videotape of another speech. Using it as a model for analysis, the class will identify the historical climate in which the speech was presented and list the areas of concern addressed in the speech, such as the nation's economy, foreign policy, and domestic issues.

4. Divided into small groups (3-4 students each) students select other speeches (from the notebook) for in-depth reading/viewing and discussion. After analyzing the speech using the criteria established in activity 1, groups report on their discussion. The class speculates as to why each speaker selected particular topics to emphasize.

5. The classroom teacher explains the requirements for the oral presentation, which include:
    *   select and read a speech or quotation
    *   locate biographical information about the speaker using library resources

- locate information about the historical context of the speech
- locate anecdotal information about the speaker or the speech
- write an oral presentation using the information collected
- present the selection and the information gathered
- (optional) memorize the selection and recite it to the class.

The library media specialist reviews the task, the importance of developing an information seeking strategy, and library resources that will assist students in developing an information search strategy.

6. Students design information seeking strategies, locate resources, and access needed information. A field trip to the public library can be planned for additional resources.

7. Students compile a notebook containing all work completed during the unit.

8. Students present information to the class in the form of an oral report, which is evaluated by the library media specialist, classroom teacher and students.

Evaluation:
Students are evaluated based on:
> participation in group discussions and related activities
> completeness of notebooks
> oral presentations.

Resources/Bibliography:
Bartlett, John. *Familiar Quotations.* Boston: Little, Brown and Company, 1980.

Bohle, Bruce. *The Home Book of American Quotations.* New York: Dodd, Mead and Company, 1967.

Boorstin, Daniel J. *An American Primer.* Chicago: University of Chicago Press, 1966.

Brussell, Eugene E. *Dictionary of Quotable Definitions.* Englewood Cliffs: Prentice-Hall, 1970.

Facsimilies of historical documents from the U.S. Archives.

Fadiman, Clifton. *The Little, Brown Book of Anecdotes.* Boston: Little, Brown and Company, 1985.

"If You Were President." *Junior Scholastic Magazine.* January 13, 1989. p. 5.

Hart, James D. *The Oxford Companion to American Literature.* New York: Oxford University Press, 1965.

Literary History of the United States: History. London: Macmillan, 1963.

Martin Luther King "I Have a Dream." (video), MPI Home Video.

Patrick, John J. and Remy, Richard C. *Civics for America.* Glenview: Scott, Foresman and Company, 1986.

Peterson, Houston. *A Treasury of the World's Great Speeches.* New York: Simon & Schuster, 1965.

Wallis, Charles L. *Our American Heritage.* New York: Harper & Row, 1970.

Webster's New Biographical Dictionary. Springfield: Merriam-Webster, 1983.

Who Was Who In America. Chicago: Marquis Publications, 1968.

Conclusion

Each of the Big Six Skills is incorporated within the scope of this integrated instructional unit. However, the ability to demonstrate evaluation skills is a key to student success. The library media specialist and teacher are careful to incorporate an evaluative component, whether formal or informal, for each activity. At the end of the unit, an evaluation of the final product is completed, not only by the library media specialist and the teacher, but also by the students. Adding this assessment activity reinforces the importance of evaluation in the information problem-solving process.– ME/RB

Thematic Statements:
Using Quotes to Understand Theme

Glenn Johnson, Library
Media Specialist
State College Area
Jr. High School
State College, PA 16803

Jerry Pitarresi
English Teacher
Ralph W. Perry
Jr. High School
New Hartford, NY 13413

*Envisioned as a cooperative effort by the library media specialist and the English teacher, this instructional unit teaches students that effective use of library media resources can help them be successful in the classroom. The unit touches on each of the Big Six Skills and is an example of how the information problem-solving process can be easily integrated into the content area curriculum. This unit was jointly designed at Ralph Perry Jr. High School by Glenn Johnson and Jerry Pitarresi. Glenn has since moved to State College (PA) Junior High School .
– ME/RB*

Unit Summary

Audience: English 9

Overview:
Students were asked to read an *outside* book, and prepare a 3-5 minute oral report. In conjunction with their reading, they were taught the use of books of quotations, e.g. Bartlett's *Familiar Quotations*, *Oxford Dictionary of Quotations*, Stevenson's *Home Book of Quotations* and others. As a culminating activity, students were asked to find a quote that acted as a thematic statement for one of the book's major concerns. They then used the quote as an opening statement and unifying element for an oral report on the book. Students were asked to identify, where possible, the speaker of the quote, and provide background information about the speaker.

Rationale:
Using quotes in written and oral communication, and identification of the effective use of themes in a story, are difficult but important tasks. The inclusion of these skills in one lesson aids in teaching both.

Content Area Objectives:
1.   To have students read a book of their own choosing for enrichment.
2.   To give students practice in speaking before groups.
3.   To give students practice in identifying thematic statements in both books and quotations.

4. To have students learn how to use quotation sources, their different arrangements and indexes.
5. To acquaint students with some famous speakers and writers through quotation sources.

Big Six Skills Objectives:

Task Definition
Students will demonstrate the ability to define the basic themes from a book they have read.

Information Seeking Strategies
Students will demonstrate the ability to identify appropriate search terms from the identified themes in order to use quotation source indexes.

Location and Access
Students will demonstrate the ability to use quotation source indexes in order to access appropriate quotes.

Use of Information
Students will demonstrate the ability to determine the appropriateness of the quote to the identified theme from the novel.

Synthesis
Students will demonstrate the ability to connect the subject of a quote to their own oral presentation, using it to help develop and elaborate a prominent theme in the novel.

Evaluation
Students will demonstrate the ability to evaluate the appropriate use of their own quotes and those of their peers through class discussion of both the novel and the quotation following each student's presentation.

Unit Organization:

lesson	accountability	location	Big Six Skills	S. A. Obj.
1	Teacher	Classroom		1
2 - 3	LMS (teacher assists)	LMC	1, 2, 3, 4	3, 4, 5
4	Teacher	Classroom	4	
5 - 9	Teacher	Classroom	5, 6	2

Key:

C	= Classroom
T	= Teacher
LMC	= Library Media Center
LMS	= Library Media Specialist
S.A. Obj.	= Subject Area Objectives
Big Six Skills	= Library & Information Skills
1	= task definition
2	= information seeking strategies
3	= location and access
4	= use of information
5	= synthesis
6	= evaluation

Activities and Materials

Period 1 Activities:
General discussion of the assignment and its purpose.
Students choose an outside reading book and sign teacher's list.
(at least one week interim for reading)

Periods 2 & 3 Activities:
Review and discuss previously learned information about themes in literature and thematic statements.
Demonstrate the use of various quotation sources through their indexes.
Stress the importance of a variety of search strategies.
Guided practice in the use of quotation sources.
Students use the library independently to find quotes.

Period 4 Activities:
Review bibliography style sheet so that sources may be cited correctly.

Periods 5 - 9 Activities:
Oral presentations by students.
Brief teacher-led discussion of books read and appropriateness of related quotes.

Evaluation:
Teacher assigns a grade to the student's presentation based on:
1. clarity and organization of the oral presentation
2. the content of the presentation identifying themes and thematic statements
3. the appropriateness of the quote as related to identified themes
4. proper use of bibliographic citations.

Follow-up/Supplemental Activities:

1. Have a number of students prepare a bulletin board advertising the book they have read using the quotes selected.

2. Have students include a quotation in a persuasive writing assignment.

3. Assign students to find a quote that relates to the next book the class reads together. Share the quotes chosen to represent themes from the same story. An interesting discussion could then ensue about selection criteria, subject meanings and *fit* in language.

Conclusion

From the library media specialist's perspective, this instructional unit is a major component of the library media program in 9th-grade. The unit gives students an excellent opportunity to review each of the Big Six Skills prior to leaving the junior high school. The library media specialist can easily assess students' information problem-solving skills and remediate as necessary. Additionally, through well-structured activities, students extend their knowledge of specialized reference sources. This unit takes advantage of high-interest content area topics and can act as a model for other major library & information skills instructional units. – ME/RB

Global Problems

Marcia Eggleston
Norwood-Norfolk
Central School
Massena,
NY
13662

Marcia Eggleston, library media specialist with the Norwood-Norfolk Central School District in upstate New York, teaches "Global Issues" as a major unit within her instructional program. As part of the 10th-grade curriculum, this is a "Big Six Skills Bonanza" unit that is used to prepare students for more involved integrated units taught in the 11th and 12th grades. The "Global Problems" unit incorporates three curricular areas: social studies, English, and library & information skills. The primary Big Six Skills objectives are information seeking strategies, use of information, synthesis, and evaluation. – ME/RB

Unit Summary

Audience: 10th Grade

Overview:
This unit of study is integrated with both social studies and English. Students are given grades in each content area. The assignment is a research report that includes review and practice of bibliography preparation, notetaking, thesis development, outlining and writing skills. Each step of the process is monitored and evaluated by the subject teacher before students proceed to the next step.

Rationale:
By researching a global problem, students learn more about the world around them, and how to think analytically about global issues. Using a term-paper format reinforces the information problem-solving process.

Content Area Objectives:
At the end of the unit, students will be able to:
1. Select and limit an appropriate topic.
2. Use and refer to both primary and secondary sources, including references from interlibrary loan sources.
3. Select, organize, and integrate information to support a central idea.
4. Compose a coherent, logical sentence or topic outline that reflects the organization of the research paper.
5. Use complete documentation in correct format.
6. Present information in an objective manner.

Major Big Six Skills Objectives:

Information Seeking Strategies
Students will design an information seeking strategy which incorporates the use of multiple sources including interlibrary loan.

Use of Information
Students will demonstrate notetaking skills.

Synthesis
Students will formulate a thesis question based on the information they access.

Evaluation
Students will evaluate the effectiveness of the information used to prove or disprove their thesis question.

Unit Organization:

lesson	time frame	accountability	location	Big Six Skills
1	40 minutes	T	C	1
2	15 minutes	LMS	C	1
3	40 minutes	LMS	LMC	1 & 2
4	40 minutes	LMS	LMC	1 & 2
5 - 9	40 min. ea.	LMS/T	LMC	3, 4, 5, & 6
10	40 minutes	LMS/T	LMC	5
11	40 minutes	T	C	6

Key:

C	= Classroom
T	= Teacher
LMC	= Library Media Center
LMS	= Library Media Specialist
Big Six Skills	= Library & Information Skills
1	= task definition
2	= information seeking strategies
3	= location and access
4	= use of information
5	= synthesis
6	= evaluation

Activities and Materials

Activities:
Students are given a list of topics from which to choose. They have two weeks to look for information and declare a topic. Students take notes and maintain a working bibliography. Each student will formulate a thesis question based on the information he/she have found. They develop an outline based on that information, and prepare rough and final drafts of their term paper. Additionally, throughout the unit, students keep track of their information seeking strategies in a log or diary.

Evaluation:
The library media specialist confers with each student regarding the Big Six Skills. Attention is paid to personal information problem-solving styles.

Students receive a grade in English based on process and format, and a grade in social studies based on content.

Conclusion

At first glance, this may seem like a typical library unit that results in a research paper. However, a unique component is added in the consultation between the library media specialist and the student. The effort to discuss information problem-solving strategies and styles as part of evaluation facilitates the development of students' library & information skills abilities. Process is as important as content. In this unit, the three teachers (English, social studies, and library media) all emphasize to students the value of having an effective and efficient approach to solving information problems. – ME/RB

Que Pasa? What's Up in Spanish-Speaking Countries of the Western Hemisphere?

Patsy Robertson,
Library Media
Specialist
Greece Athena
High School
Rochester, NY
14610

The foreign language curriculum offers many opportunities for integrated instruction. Patsy Robertson, library media specialist in Rochester, NY, shares one of the many units she teaches in co-ordination with her foreign language teachers. Although students are engaged in a full range of library & information skills activities, the primary areas of concern from a Big Six Skills perspective are information seeking strategies and synthesis. This particular unit can easily be adapted for any foreign language, at a range of grade levels.
– ME/RB

Unit Summary

Audience: Spanish III (Grades 10-12)

Overview:
This unit combines the objectives from Spanish III with library & information skills as well as encourages cooperative learning and shared responsibility.

Working in small groups, students research current issues and events related to Spanish-speaking countries of the Western Hemisphere, and create a newspaper to share with classmates.

Rationale:
It is valuable for students to learn about Spanish-speaking countries in the Western Hemisphere. Cooperative learning reinforces different learning styles and shared responsibility. Creation of a newspaper allows for a unique sharing of information.

Content Area Objectives:
1.   To learn about current events/issues (such as social, political, economic, en-vironmental, life-styles, relationship with the United States) that affect citi-zens of Spanish-speaking countries in the Western Hemisphere.

2.   To practice writing skills in Spanish.

Big Six Skills Objectives:

Task Definition
Identify potential issues and events.

Information Seeking Strategies
Determine appropriate sources of information.

Location and Access
Locate background information on a country.

Use of Information
Determine usefulness of information for project.

Synthesis
Combine information from various sources.
Prepare the newspaper.

Evaluation
Determine if the newspaper meets the assigned requirements.

Unit Organization:

Periods	Place	Activity	Accountability	Big Six Skills
1.5	C	1,2	T	1, 2, 3
1.5	LMC	3, 4	LMS	2, 3
1.0	LMC	5	S	3, 4
.5	LMC	6	S	3
3.0	LMC	7	S	3, 4, 5
1.0	LMC	8	LMS	5
	LMC or C	9	S	5, 6

Key:

C	= Classroom
T	= Teacher
LMC	= Library Media Center
LMS	= Library Media Specialist
S	= Student
Big Six Skills	= Library & Information Skills
1	= task definition
2	= information seeking strategies
3	= location and access
4	= use of information
5	= synthesis
6	= evaluation

Activities and Material

Activities:
1. Introduce unit; present guidelines for content and timelines; select groups and countries.
2. Discuss types of information needed. Have students list the questions they need to answer.
3. Have students summarize their questions and create a list of possible sources.
4. Review the use of appropriate reference sources based on students' lists.
5. Initiate research and writing.
6. Provide instruction in the use of additional sources as needed.
7. Monitor research and writing.
8. Present sample newspapers created with newspaper computer software (e.g., *Newsroom*); instruct in the use of *Newsroom*.
9. Oversee production of the newspapers.

Evaluation:

Evaluation is based on:
> students' search strategy
> observation of students' use of the LMC
> student created newspaper
> teacher and library media specialist review of the product (both quality and content).

Materials:
chalkboard
overhead projector with Datashow
multiple copies of *Newsroom* or equivalent software.

Supplemental Activity:
Provide Spanish language newspapers for student use.

Conclusion

Students who are involved in guided practice of library & information skills become more competent at solving information problems. This instructional unit provides an opportunity for students to practice previously learned Spanish language skills. It also gives the library media specialist and classroom teacher a chance to review and reinforce the Big Six Skills. This unit is successful because it gives students the opportunity to organize and present researched information in a creative and interesting format. Students expand their synthesis skills through the use of computers and specialized software.– ME/RB

The Family: Issues and Answers

Robert E. Berkowitz,
Library Media Specialist,
with
Eileen Schwartz,
Social Studies Teacher,
and
Corrine Robideau,
Art Teacher
Wayne Central High
School
Ontario Center, NY
14520

"The Family: Issues and Answers" was designed as a major unit of instruction within the social studies curriculum at Wayne Central High School in Ontario Center, NY. Students complete this unit at the end of a half year course in Sociology. The unit acts as a culminating activity that requires students to apply general concepts and skills to a specific topic in sociology. Students present the results of their information problem-solving effort in three different formats: written, oral and visual. From a Big Six Skills perspective, this unit provides students with an opportunity to review and polish-up their information problem-solving abilities. This unit was cooperatively designed, developed and taught by the library media specialist (co-author Bob Berkowitz), a social studies teacher, Eileen Schwartz, and an art teacher, Corrine Robideau. This integrated instructional unit is presented with its various worksheets and other related materials.– ME/RB

Unit Summary

Audience: Sociology (Grades 11-12)

Overview:
This 4- week unit of study is an integrated library & information skills curriculum and sociology curriculum unit that also includes an art component.

Because the unit acts as the culminating unit for the concepts learned within the scope of the sociology curriculum, it comes at the end of the course.

Society relies on the family for many vital functions. This unit provides students with the opportunity to extend their knowledge of family, social relationships, and human interaction within the context of society. Students extend beyond classroom experience in order to gain knowledge and insight into a range of issues that focus on family. They share that information with fellow classmates in a variety of formats.

Rationale:
The library & information skills, sociology and art curricula share a common goal: to teach students to successfully solve information problems using appropriate information resources. When students successfully complete this unit of study,

they will have reviewed and reinforced the library & information skills associated with information problem-solving. These lifelong skills, integral to the sociology course content, are skills that are transferable to other courses within the social studies curriculum, as well as other content areas such as art.

General Objectives:
1. To review and remediate the information problem-solving process within the context of the sociology course content.

2. To extend students' knowlege of family, social relationships, and human interaction though information resources available in the high school library media center.

3. To provide students with a positive learning experience in the library media center.

Sociology Content Objectives:
1. Students will extend their knowledge and interest in the topics assigned through purposeful reading of current non-textbook information sources.

2. Students will become aware of the various aspects, causes, and alternative solutions to family issues.

3. Students will demonstrate the ability to explain the issues and alternatives related to their topic in a logical manner, based on fact rather than opinion.

4. Students will reinforce and extend the general concepts learned thoughout the course.

Big Six Skills Objectives:

Task Definition
    Define assignment.
    Determine information needs.

Information Seeking Strategies
    Identify possible sources of information.

Location and Access
    Locate resources from a range of materials.
    Access information to meet the needs of the defined tasks.

Use of Information
    Determine the relevance of obtained information to meet the assigned tasks.
    Analyze accessed information.

Synthesis
Organize and share information/findings in written, visual, and oral formats.

Evaluation
Evaluate products and processes.

Unit Organization:

period	accountability	location	Big Six Skills
1	T	C	1
1	LMS	C	1, 2, 3
2	LMS & T & students	LMC	3, 4, 5, 6
3	students	LMC/other	3, 4, 5, 6
[two weeks]			
4	Art Teacher	C	1, 4, 5, 6
5 +	T	C	5, 6

Key:

C	= Classroom	
T	= Teacher	
LMC	= Library Media Center	
LMS	= Library Media Specialist	
Big Six Skills	= Library & Information Skills	
1	= task definition	
2	= information seeking strategies	
3	= location and access	
4	= use of information	
5	= synthesis	
6	= evaluation	

Planning Time:
- 1 period - review and set schedule
- additional consultation time as needed

Activities and Materials

Period 1 Activities:
1. Give assignment to students, and carefully review the major requirements.

2. Assign students topics from the predetermined list. Distribute folders containing the basic worksheets and one article (specific to their topic) for review.

3.   Discuss the information problem-solving process: the Big Six Skills.

4.   Review the potential resources appropriate to meet the assigned task.

Period 2 Activities:
5.   Review assignment requirements. Review and evaluate completed article analysis.

Period 3 Activities:
6.   Students conduct library media center research - to locate eight citations, and access four sources of information on the assigned topic.

7.   Students read the information accessed and complete response sheets (homework/study hall time available).

Period 4 Activities:
8.   The art teacher reviews the poster task and discusses techniques of poster design.

9.   Students continue research and presentation preparation.

Period 5 - 7 Activities: (beginning date assigned by the classroom teacher)
10. Students submit research papers, present findings orally, and display posters in the library media center.

11. Content area teacher and the library media specialist review and evaluate the research results and process.

12. The content area teacher and the art teacher review and evaluate the posters.

Evaluation:
Student work is evaluated on both a formal and an informal basis. This allows the sociology teacher, art teacher, and library media specialist to reinforce or redirect students' research efforts so that students' success will be maximized.

Formal Evaluation:
1.   written multiple source research paper (5 pages)   = 25%
2.   oral presentation/information sharing (5-10 minutes)   = 25%
3.   poster/visual presentation   = 25%
4.   on time and completeness   = 25%

Materials:
1. assignment sheet with tasks and deadlines
2. preselected article for guided practice in the use of the article analysis sheet
3. article analysis sheets
4. multiple source paper evaluation form
5. oral presentation evaluation sheets
6. visual presentation - poster design sheet
7. 1 file folder for each student

Resources/Bibliography:
Selected *Social Issues Resources Series (SIRS)* documents
Text on Microfilm (TOM), Information Access Company
Readers' Guide, H.W. Wilson
Magazine Articles Summary (MAS) EBSCO Electronic Information
Journal articles
Various resources from the vertical file

**Instructional materials supporting this unit are provided
on the next five pages.**

Poster Design

A good poster design combines a *visual image* with a *written message*.

Subject: Identify and think about the idea you wish to present. Your poster should inspire people. A unique idea or approach can be very successful providing it *directly relates* to your subject.

Checklist For Poster Design

- What medium or materials are you using?

- What size and shape is your poster? The design must relate to the size and shape.

- When in doubt, keep the design simple. Too many colors, too much lettering, and too many images can confuse the viewer and scramble your message.

- Does your lettering relate to the poster design?

- Does it have visual emphasis or impact?

- Is there unity in your design?

- Have you used color or value to improve and contribute to your design?

- Does the design have balance?

- Are all the words spelled correctly?

Suggested Approach: Sketch out all of your ideas before deciding on a final design. Refine your best idea and check it against the above list.

Name: _____ Teacher: _____

Date: _____ Class: _____ Period: _____

Title: _____

The Family: Issues and Answers - Document Analysis Sheet

Cite the information source using the proper bibliographic form:

_____

_____

_____

After reading the information carefully, complete the following form:

Identify and quote or restate the thesis statement.

_____

_____

_____

_____

Select five key words that are important to understanding this information, list them, and define each word using dictionary or encyclopedia.

1._____

2._____

3._____

4._____

5._____

page 2

Select three main ideas or facts that the author uses to support his or her thesis. List and rank them according to their importance. Explain your rationale for the ranking.

Underline the section of the document where the author states his or her conclusion. In your own words, using no more than three sentences, restate the author's conclusion.

Name: _____ Teacher: _____

Date: _____ Class: _____ Period: _____

Title: _____

The Family: Issues and Answers - Final Evaluation Form

Outstanding	Very Good	Good	Unacceptable	
❏	❏	❏	❏	1. Clearly stated thesis
❏	❏	❏	❏	2. Clear pattern of organization
❏	❏	❏	❏	3. Provides appropriate specific references
❏	❏	❏	❏	4. Explains significance of quotes and facts used
❏	❏	❏	❏	5. Makes appropriate generalizations
❏	❏	❏	❏	6. Uses pertinent information (i.e., reasons, facts, details, examples) to support thesis
❏	❏	❏	❏	7. Has logical conclusions
❏	❏	❏	❏	8. Contains sufficient amount of scientific evidence
❏	❏	❏	❏	9. Report has good style: smoothness, transition, coherence
❏	❏	❏	❏	10. Footnotes are appropriate, and in correct form
❏	❏	❏	❏	11. Bibliography includes a minimum of 5 sources
❏	❏	❏	❏	12. All Document Analysis Sheets and Document Synthesis Sheets attached

Comments:

Name: _____ Teacher: _____

Date: _____ Class: _____ Period: _____

Title: _____

The Family: Issues and Answers - Oral Presentation Evaluation Form

Outstanding	Very Good	Good	Adequate	Unacceptable	
❏	❏	❏	❏	❏	1. Introduction which clearly states purpose
❏	❏	❏	❏	❏	2. Organization of information
❏	❏	❏	❏	❏	3. Properly documented sources
❏	❏	❏	❏	❏	4. Clear and direct presentation of information
❏	❏	❏	❏	❏	5. Clear understanding of the topic
❏	❏	❏	❏	❏	6. Appropriate use of visuals
❏	❏	❏	❏	❏	7. Question and Answer segment
❏	❏	❏	❏	❏	8. General preparation for presentation

Comments:

Conclusion

Students who participate in this guided research activity enjoy the opportunity to share their discoveries in different formats. By having every student create an art project, a written report, and an oral presentation, each student is given the chance to find a hidden talent. Being required to effectively communicate the same information in multiple ways also forces students to reconsider their topics. In terms of evaluation, the content teacher can assess student knowledge of course content, the art teacher can review their products, and the library media specialist can evaluate their information problem-solving skills. All of this occurs in a culminating study of the major concepts taught in the course. -ME/RB

Chapter 6
Generic Lessons

The ultimate goal of instruction in the Big Six Skills is to provide students with the abilities necessary to solve a variety of information problems. As previously stated, the Big Six Skills approach is applicable to all situations that require an information-based solution. Such broad transferability and generalizability offer both an opportunity and a challenge. The opportunity is to enhance students' abilities through a wide range of situations; the challenge is to design meaningful instructional experiences for those situations.

Generic lessons are an effective way to provide such meaningful instructional experiences. A generic lesson is an instructional effort that guides students through a specific Big Six Skills' objective. The lesson is often designed around a generic device (e.g., a checklist of potential sources) or a strategy (e.g., a method for notetaking). Students learn to use the devices and strategies as part of the Big Six Skills approach. After students have successfully worked through a generic device or strategy, they can adopt, modify, or design their own. Hopefully, students will ultimately incorporate an assortment of devices and strategies as part of their personal approaches to solving information problems.

Generic lessons are only effective when integrated with subject area instruction. The subject area context provides the purpose and motivation for learning. Generic lessons are useful because they are flexible and easily adapted to different subject area curriculum situations. Without the subject area connection, generic lessons are as inappropriate as any other attempt to teach library & information skills in isolation.

In addition to the curriculum context, it is also important to present every generic lesson within the overall Big Six Skills context. One strength of the Big Six Skills approach is its emphasis on process. Individual skills and actions are applied within the overall process of information problem-solving. Although the intent of a generic lesson may be to develop a specific skill, students should always be aware of its relationship to the general Big Six Skills framework.

A wide variety of generic lessons can be designed for each of the Big Six Skills. What follows are sample generic devices and activities that you can add to your own repertoire.

Task Definition

Recognizing that information is required to solve a problem or make a decision is the first step in information problem-solving. *Task definition* is defined as determining the purpose and need for information. One generic strategy for helping students to develop the ability to clearly define tasks is to teach them to focus on key *task* words used by teachers. The result will be a clearer understanding of the task and its requirements from an information perspective.

A task definition generic lesson based on the worksheet on the following page focuses attention on task requirements for common key words. The library media specialist or the teacher can review the key word definitions with students and discuss their relationships to tasks.

Simple in concept, the worksheet has value whenever students need to clarify tasks. The key words often appear on assignment sheets and essay questions. Teachers frequently use these terms in explaining what they want students to do. Students who can define these words and apply the definitions to the immediate situation can better understand the intent of the assignment, and therefore better meet its requirements. This generic lesson can be successfully applied in most subject areas.

It is important to emphasize that this worksheet should not be the basis for an isolated library skills lesson. It should only be used in the context of an actual subject area curriculum situation.

Task Definition: **Key Words Define Tasks**

Name: _____ Subject: _____

Unit of Study: _____

Topic: _____

Task: _____

Key words are very important because key words tell you what to do. Some key words often found in assignments and questions are:

Analyze:
Divide the topic into parts. Tell how each part is related to the topic. Also, tell how each part is related to the part that comes before and the part that comes after.

Assess:
Rate or evaluate something.

Compare:
Decide how things are the same and different. Tell about both the similarities and differences.

Contrast:
Find differences between things and tell about the differences.

Define:
Explain what it means. Tell how it is like some things and different than others.

Describe:
Tell all you can, in an organized way.

Discuss:
Determine what the different sides are and tell about them. Discuss is similar to Describe.

Evaluate:
Give the positive and negative points, advantages and disadvantages, pros and cons. Also give your opinion.

Explain:
Clearly tell the details about something, or the reasons or causes for something.

Illustrate:
Describe specific examples. The more examples you can give, the better.

Relate:
Tell how things are connected, what they have in common.

Summarize:
Present your information in as few words as possible (and in your own words).

Information Seeking Strategies

Introduction:

Information seeking strategies is defined as examining alternative approaches for acquiring appropriate information to meet a defined task. Recognizing, selecting, and prioritizing potential sources of information are all part of information seeking strategies. A checklist is a useful instructional device for carrying out these activities.

The *Resources Checklist* on the next page is an example of a simple instructional device for working on information seeking strategies. Used as the foundation for a generic lesson on information seeking strategies, the checklist is applicable to any unit in social studies, language arts, science, health, careers, or any other subject area that requires students to use multiple resources for a given report, paper, project, presentation, or product.

In the lesson, the library media specialist can help students to narrow the range of possible types of sources appropriate to the task. Students can make special notes on the checklist based on comments by the library media specialist and their teacher. The checklist can also serve as a summary sheet as the students continue the information problem-solving process.

The level of sophistication and scope of the checklist is highly flexible. Some library media specialists may choose to develop one general checklist for all situations; others may create variations based on grade level and/or subject area. Either approach can be effective when targeted to meeting needs associated with a specific subject area need.

Information Seeking Strategies: Resources Checklist

Name:_____ Subject:_____

Unit of Study:_____

Topic:_____

Task:_____

1) Check appropriate sources.
2) List specifics.
3) Determine availability.

Primary Sources:
☐ Eyewitness:_____
☐ Experiment:_____
☐ Observation:_____
☐ Other(e.g., video):_____
☐ Historic Document:_____

Secondary Sources:
☐ Books (Nonfiction):_____
☐ Books (Fiction):_____
☐ Dictionary:_____
☐ Encyclopedia:_____
☐ Atlas:_____
☐ Almanac:_____
☐ Indexes:_____
☐ Vertical File:_____
☐ Newspapers:_____
☐ Video Tapes:_____
☐ Audio Tapes:_____
☐ Slide/Tape:_____
☐ Filmstrips:_____
☐ Special Online:_____
☐ Other:_____
☐ Other:_____

Location and Access

Location and access involves locating a range of information sources to meet a defined task, and the ability to find information. The following worksheet can be incorporated into a two-part generic lesson that emphasizes both location and access skills. The lesson first directs students to relevant sections of the library media center. Students can circle areas on the library media center map containing resources selected as priorities from information seeking strategies.

The second part of the lesson guides students to more effective access within resources. The objective is to develop extended vocabularies for key word searching. The library media specialist and/or the teacher can work with students to identify the overall topic to be searched, subtopics, and synonyms for the subtopics.

Instruction in location and access is not always exciting. However, students do respond positively when the lesson will assist them in meeting real needs. This is accomplished by linking both parts of the lesson to specific subject area activities that involve library media resources.

Location:	In the Library Media Center
Access:	To Information Within Resources

Location:

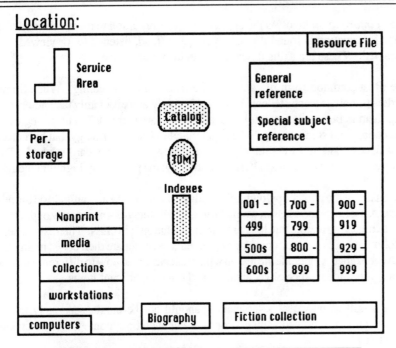

Access: Keyword Searching

The key to access within a resource is the <u>vocabulary</u>. The following exercise will help to develop a rich vocabulary for searching on a particular topic.

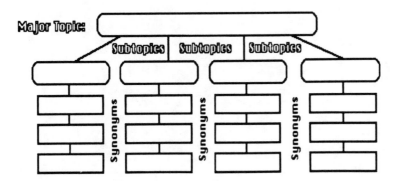

Use of Information

Use of information involves the application of information to meet a defined task. Once information is found it must be engaged (read, listened to, or viewed) and extracted. These are skills fundamental to information use.

The most common form of extracting information is notetaking. When library media specialists teach students how to effectively and efficiently take notes, they help them to be more successful students. There are many different strategies for notetaking, and students should be encouraged to find the strategy that best meets their needs. The most commonly taught strategy is the notecard method. This generic lesson is based on an alternative strategy: the photocopy/highlight method.

The basics of the photocopy/highlight method of notetaking are outlined on the next page. A useful generic lesson would be to give all students a photocopy of the same article related to a topic that they are currently studying in class. Then ask students to follow steps 2 - 4. Upon completion, students can compare their coded main ideas with each other. Conclude the lesson with a discussion on how to differentiate main ideas, minor ideas, special vocabulary, and other significant items.

Even a skill as universal as notetaking should not be taught separately from a distinct curriculum need. Integration will enhance both content and notetaking objectives.

Use of Information: Photocopy/Highlight Notetaking Method

There are many approaches to notetaking. One of the most useful is the Photocopy/ Highlight method (sometimes called the Xerox-Underline method). The Photocopy/Highlight method can:

- focus your attention on main points
- show the organizational pattern of the information
- note specialized vocabulary
- save time.

The Photocopy/Highlight system has four aspects:

- copy
- highlight
- circle
- code.

The last three tasks can be done concurrently to create combinations that will personalize the system for your special needs.

1. Copy: *Make a photocopy* of the relevant magazine article, book passage, or section from a reference work.

2. Highlight: *Highlight* or underline the main-idea sentences or phrases, thesis statement, supporting evidence, and key words. This technique is valuable in that it forces you to identify the ideas that are important. Highlighting also helps when information needs to be reviewed quickly. It is also important not to underline too much. Don't highlight every sentence. If that happens, it becomes difficult to differentiate between main ideas and minor points.

3. Circle: *Circle* large portions of important text. Often there will be large blocks of important information. Using the highlight technique in this situation may not be appropriate. Circles, however, can be used effectively. Use circles to note large portions of text, diagrams or charts that contain major concepts, explanations or examples.

4. Code: *Design a coding system* of stars, Xs, exclamation points or other marks that can be written in the margins. Coding information, in addition to underlining, makes it is easier to review. Simply follow the code to pick out main ideas, minor ideas, examples, or important vocabulary words. The code signs will help to focus attention on the important information in the reading.

The Photocopy/Highlight notetaking method can help you use information more effectively and efficiently. This simple approach to notetaking will help you extract information and add value to the information source.

Synthesis

Synthesis is defined as the integration of information drawn from multiple sources. Synthesis includes both the organization as well as the presentation of information.

This generic lesson focuses attention on determining the best ways to present information for a given situation. The sample worksheet can be used to:

- explain (or review if previously discussed) the features and characteristics of certain presentation modes

- discuss being discriminating *consumers* of various presentations

- consider the presentation format(s) best suited to communicating certain types of information (e.g., trends, arguments, how-to, facts)

- assist students in making decisions for their own presentations.

Lessons on any of these can be tailored to the requirements of specific subject area units. The degree of detail will depend on the grade levels of the students and the time available for the lessons.

Synthesis:	Product/Project Checklist

Name:_____   Subject:_____

Unit of Study:_____

Topic:_____

Task:_____

(1) Determine the major category for your presentation.
(2) Select the formats that meet the requirements of the assignment.
(3) Check the formats you are most interested in doing.
(4) Compare your results for steps 2 and 3, choose one format, or create a combination of formats.
(5) Let the library media specialist and teacher know what presentation format you have chosen.

Written:
☐ Activity Center
☐ Advertisement
☐ Bibliography
☐ Biography
☐ Booklet
☐ Character Sketch
☐ Crossword Puzzle
☐ Dictionary
☐ Game
☐ Greeting Cards
☐ Interview
☐ Letter
☐ Log
☐ Magazine
☐ Newspaper Article
☐ Newspaper
☐ Outline
☐ Play
☐ Poem
☐ Questionnaire
☐ Story
☐ Survey
☐ Test
☐ Travel Brochure
☐ Word Search
☐ Written Report
☐ Other: _____

Visual:
☐ Advertisement
☐ Badges
☐ Bumperstickers
☐ Banner
☐ Bulletin Board
☐ Cartoon
☐ Chart
☐ Collage
☐ Dance
☐ Diagram
☐ Diorama
☐ Display
☐ Drawing
☐ Filmstrip
☐ Graph
☐ Map Collection
☐ Mask
☐ Model
☐ Pantomime
☐ Painting
☐ Papier-mache
☐ Photographs
☐ Poster
☐ Scrapbook
☐ Slide Show
☐ Transparency
☐ Other: _____

Oral:
☐ Audio Tape Recording
☐ Crackerbarrel
☐ Debate
☐ Dialog
☐ Dramatization
☐ Interview
☐ Oral Report
☐ Panel Discussion
☐ Play
☐ Puppet Show
☐ Skit
☐ Song
☐ Speech
☐ Story
☐ Other: _____

Combinations
☐ Game
☐ Interactive Video
☐ Slide-Tape Show
☐ Video: _____
☐ Other: _____
☐ Other: _____

Evaluation

Evaluation focuses students' attention on making judgments, based on a set of pre-established criteria. It is important that students make two judgments: (1) determine how effectively the original task, as defined, was met, and (2) assess the efficiency of the entire information problem-solving process. Evaluation teaches students that both the end (i.e., the quality of their solution to an information problem) as well as the means (their personal information problem-solving skills) are important.

A generic instrument designed to assess the information problem-solving process is presented on the next page. One possible generic lesson would be to have students brainstorm criteria for assessment for each of the Big Six Skills. Another more individualized approach would be to incorporate the worksheet as part of a project or report requirement. It could then be reviewed by the teacher or library media specialist in a personal interview with each student.

Evaluation is clearly tied to the requirements of subject area curricula. This lesson would be meaningless if not tied to a curriculum need.

Evaluation: Checklist

Name: _____   Subject: _____

Unit of Study : _____

Topic : _____

Task : _____

_____

_____

	start date	finish date	student eval.	LMS/T eval.
Task Definition:				
Information Seeking Strategies:				
Location and Access:				
Use of Information:				
Synthesis:				
Evaluation:				

Use the following scale to evaluate how well you used your time during this assignment.

1 _____ 2 _____ 3 _____ 4 _____ 5
wasted   very well

Explain your answer below.

Generic Lesson Outline

Each of the preceding lessons targeted one of the Big Six Skills. Sometimes, it is valuable to cover the entire information problem-solving process in one lesson. This final generic lesson demonstrates how to present the overall Big Six Skills approach linked to a specific curriculum requirement.

A very common assignment is to require students to answer questions at the end of a textbook chapter or from a handout. This assignment is found in all grades and most subjects. The lesson outline that follows demonstrates that the Big Six Skills approach is effective and valuable even in those situations presumed to be simple information problems, situations that don't require specialized resources beyond the textbook or handout.

This lesson is presented as a straightforward lecture/discussion that can be delivered by the library media specialist or classroom teacher. It can be used the first time students are given an assignment that requires them to use their textbooks to answer a set of questions. It doesn't matter if students have previously received similar assignments, or even similar instruction in the past. Keep in mind, however, that if this is not the first time you use this lesson with a particular group of students, the focus of the discussion would change from teaching a new skill to review and remediation of a previously learned skill.

The emphasis of this generic lesson is on the broad Big Six Skills approach to information problem-solving. As previously stated, it is applicable in many different curriculum situations, in terms of content, grade level, and ability level. This lesson reinforces the fact that library media specialists can and do contribute to students' content learning. But, as with all library & information skills instruction, this generic lesson should not be taught apart from a direct information need.

Using Textbooks to Answer Questions

Materials: Textbook or assignment sheet, blackboard, overhead projector, or opaque projector.

Sequence: Review Big Six Skills with the specific assignment in mind. Isolate the specific skills, and relate them to the specific information need. Using specific examples from the students' own text, show examples of each instructional objective.

Objective: To teach students how to use a specific strategy, based on the Big Six Skills approach, to effectively and efficiently use a textbook to answer questions.

Lesson Outline:

Task Definition
Basic question: • What is the task/problem?
Answer: • The problem is to answer the questions at the back of the book (or listed on a handout).

Other concepts for discussion:
  • Students need to determine whether they are required to answer the questions in their own words or use direct quotes from the textbook.
  • Most often students are required to answer in their own words.

Information Seeking Strategies
Basic question: • What sources of information are available?
Answer: • The textbook is the fundamental source for information.

Other concepts for discussion:
  • There is a correct section/chapter within the textbook.
  • There may also be a summary at the end of the chapter.
  • Students should look for time lines, or information separated from the main text (e.g., highlighted, boxed).
  • It also may be valuable to use other information resources in coordination with the textbook (e.g., dictionary, encyclopedia, almanac, special subject dictionaries).

Location and Access
Basic question: • How do students get to the right place in the textbook as quickly as possible?
Answer: • Look for typographical aids: headings for each section in a chapter, key words in boldface or italic type, information in the margins.

Other concepts for discussion:
- There may be special sections in the book (e.g., table of contents, glossary, series of maps, tables or charts, index, appendices, illustrations).

Information Use

Basic question:
- How do students get the information they need out of a textbook?

Answer:
- Read the questions first. Students should make sure they understand the question (what is being asked for) and what they are required to do (the key words).
- Skim or scan the chapter, looking for each of the broad headings. Go back through the chapter looking for relevant information.
- When students find the information needed to answer the question, use quotes or paraphrase in their own words.

Other concepts for discussion:
- The first and last paragraphs of each section are often important places to find answers to questions.
- In many textbooks, the questions are often in the same sequence as the material.
- Students can take notes on each question before writing the answer. Use a 3x5-inch index card for each question.

Synthesis

Basic question:
- After students find the information, what do they do with it?

Answer:
- If the original task is to use their own words and students have a problem in doing so, they should read their notes and then write the answer without looking at the notes.

Other concepts for discussion:
- Students should always note the page numbers of the source of the information.
- Students should note direct quotes from the book by using quotation marks.

Evaluation

Basic questions:
- Does each question have an acceptable answer?
- How well are students doing at this assignment?
- Do they need to do anything else?

Answer:
- If necessary, they might loop back to information seeking strategies.
- Consider using a special section of the book (e.g., glossary), or other sources (e.g., encyclopedia, almanac, dictionary).

Other concepts for discussion:
- Students should consider any areas needing special assistance.
- Students should assess their notetaking, paraphrasing, and summarizing skills.
- Students can let the teacher or library media specialist know if they would like more instruction in any particular area.

Generic lessons provide a useful structure for focusing students' attention on a particular skill or component. Library media specialists are encouraged to document those strategies and devices that are particularly effective for teaching information problem-solving. Most strategies and devices are relevant to many different curriculum situations. By compiling a file of effective generic lessons, library media specialists can respond quickly to demands for targeted library & information skills instruction.

This concludes the presentation of the Big Six Skills approach. Throughout this book, we have attempted to provide both a conceptual framework and practical strategies for developing a library & information skills instructional program based on information problem-solving. The strength of the Big Six Skills approach lies in its widespread applicability. People are continually faced with a myriad of information problems. Consciously or not, they must engage in some process to resolve those problems. The Big Six Skills approach offers a general model that easily accommodates differences in style, sequence, and emphasis.

Every school setting and associated library media program is unique. Nevertheless, the Big Six Skills approach can be effective in every school setting. Implementation will likely require modifications and adaptations to meet local needs; however, the fundamentals remain the same:

- to provide students with a general model for information problem-solving

- to fully integrate library & information skills instruction with subject area curricula

- to develop each of the Big Six Skills and related components through many different integrated instructional activities (across subject areas and grade levels)

- to emphasize the value of the Big Six Skills approach in all problem situations.

The Big Six Skills approach can help the library media program fulfill its role as the center of a school's instructional effort and an individual's lifelong learning.

Appendix A

This Appendix includes the completed exercises from Chapter 3.

Exercises 1b and 1c require matching specific curriculum activities with the related Big Six Skills. A key to completing the exercises is placing the activities in a logical, sequential order. While there may be some leeway in response and interpretation, the answers reflect a consensus of opinion. If your responses differ, compare your rationales with those provided.

Exercises 2b and 2c require generating activities that relate to each of the Big Six Skills for a given curriculum situation. For these exercises, the completed responses should only be viewed as examples of a range of possible answers.

Exercise 1b.

Objectives

To match each of the activities (in the first column) with the appropriate Big Six Skill (in the second column) and explain your reasons for doing so (in the third column). There is one activity for each of the Big Six Skills.

Situation

Students in a 6th-grade class* are working on vocabulary. The students are given a list of 15 terms to define in their own words. The teacher requires that students note the source for each definition, including page numbers if appropriate.

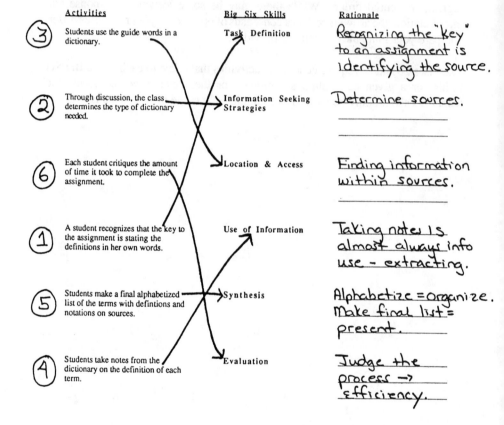

Activities	Big Six Skills	Rationale
③ Students use the guide words in a dictionary.	Task Definition	Recognizing the "key" to an assignment is identifying the source.
② Through discussion, the class determines the type of dictionary needed.	Information Seeking Strategies	Determine sources.
⑥ Each student critiques the amount of time it took to complete the assignment.	Location & Access	Finding information within sources.
① A student recognizes that the key to the assignment is stating the definitions in her own words.	Use of Information	Taking notes is almost always info use - extracting.
⑤ Students make a final alphabetized list of the terms with definitions and notations on sources.	Synthesis	Alphabetize = organize. Make final list = present.
④ Students take notes from the dictionary on the definition of each term.	Evaluation	Judge the process —> efficiency.

*Although this situation is presented in a grade 6 context, it is common to many grade levels. If useful, adjust the activities to better simulate your own situation.

Exercise 1c.

Objectives

To match each of the activities (in the first column) with the appropriate Big Six Skill (in the second column) and explain your reasons for doing so (in the third column). There is one activity for each of the Big Six Skills.

Situation

Students in 11th-grade social studies are required to complete a timeline.* Given a list of 10 dates, they are to determine what happened on that date, whether the date is truly significant in U.S. history, and if so, to place the event on the proper place on the timeline.

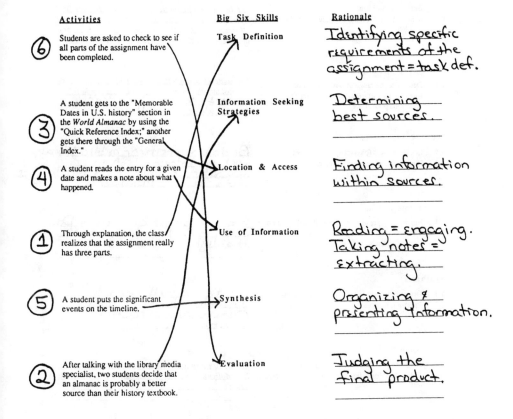

Activities	Big Six Skills	Rationale
⑥ Students are asked to check to see if all parts of the assignment have been completed.	Task Definition	Identifying specific requirements of the assignment = task def.
③ A student gets to the "Memorable Dates in U.S. history" section in the *World Almanac* by using the "Quick Reference Index;" another gets there through the "General Index."	Information Seeking Strategies	Determining best sources.
④ A student reads the entry for a given date and makes a note about what happened.	Location & Access	Finding information within sources.
① Through explanation, the class realizes that the assignment really has three parts.	Use of Information	Reading = engaging. Taking notes = extracting.
⑤ A student puts the significant events on the timeline.	Synthesis	Organizing & presenting information.
② After talking with the library media specialist, two students decide that an almanac is probably a better source than their history textbook.	Evaluation	Judging the final product.

*Again, this situation and assignment are common to many grade levels.

Exercise 2b.

Objective

For the given curriculum situation, describe one or two activities that relate to each of the Big Six Skills.

Situation

A 12th-grade economics class is studying large corporations and how to actually determine how well a company is doing. Students are to choose a company, write a profile of the company and discuss the relative value of different sources of information about the company.

Task Definition

1.1 Define the problem
1.2 Identify the information requirements of the problem

The library media specialist discusses (with the full class) the type of information needed – primary information from the company, and secondary information from analysts and others.

Information Seeking Strategies

2.1 Determine the range of possible sources
2.2 Evaluate the different possible sources to determine priorities

The students ask questions about various business-oriented information resources – print and computer. Select 3 best sources available locally.

Location and Access

3.1 Locate sources (physically and intellectually)
3.2 Find information within sources

Go to university or public library. Look up information in Standard & Poors & on line business data bases. (Dow Jones)

Use of Information

4.1 Engage (e.g., read, hear, view) the information in a source
4.2 Extract information from a source

Get a print out from Dow Jones or other data bases. Highlight relevant sections.

Synthesis

5.1 Organize information from multiple sources
5.2 Present information

Write a full report. Include charts/graphs. Create an executive summary.

Evaluation

6.1 Judge the product (effectiveness)
6.2 Judge the information problem-solving process (efficiency)

The library media specialist asks the class to discuss how difficult it was to get/use the online vs. print sources.

NOTES:

Exercise 2c.

Objective

For the given curriculum situation, describe one or two activities that relate to each of the Big Six Skills.

Situation

A 1st-grade class is studying *community* (what makes a community, people and places in their community). Each student is going to make a picture book of community helpers. Each entry in the picture book should include a picture of a community person in the appropriate setting and a sentence (or two) describing who the person is and what he or she does. The teacher gives the students information about three helpers, and the students are to add at least five on their own. The teacher also sends home an explanation sheet to parents suggesting how they can help their children.

Task Definition

1.1 Define the problem
1.2 Identify the information requirements of the problem

> The teacher & students talk about what a helper is & list a few on the board. The teacher shows the students a sample picture book so they know what they will be making.

Information Seeking Strategies

2.1 Determine the range of possible sources
2.2 Evaluate the different possible sources to determine priorities

> The LM specialist shows students the special reserve section on community helpers. The class talks about visiting places in the community.

Location and Access

3.1 Locate sources (physically and intellectually)
3.2 Find information within sources

> The students go to the LMC in small groups.
> Parents take children to the firehouse. The mayor visits the class.

Use of Information

4.1 Engage (e.g., read, hear, view) the information in a source
4.2 Extract information from a source

> The students listen to the mayor & ask questions.
> The students draw a rough sketch of the crossing guard.

Synthesis

5.1 Organize information from multiple sources
5.2 Present information

> The students decide what order they want to put their pictures in. The students put their picturebooks together.

Evaluation

6.1 Judge the product (effectiveness)
6.2 Judge the information problem-solving process (efficiency)

> The class makes a master list of all the different helpers included. Each student decides which one or two he/she would add next time.

NOTES:

Appendix B

This Appendix includes four sample curriculum maps created using an Apple Macintosh computer and Reflex database management software. All curriculum maps were generated from the same K-12 sample curriculum database.

The first map includes all K-12 units in the database that use (1) some resources beyond a textbook and (2) evaluation methods beyond a test. The map is sorted in ascending order by grade and then by subject. The map gives an overview of units that are possible candidates for Big Six Skills instruction.

The second map includes all the same data, sorted by marking period. Sorting by marking period helps in planning the skills instructional program over the year.

The third map is designed to help focus attention on potential priority units. Units that involve multiple materials and reports or products are likely candidates for integrated Big Six Skills instruction. In this database, many units meet these criteria. Two other variables, number of students and number of periods, may help to further determine priorities.* Therefore, the map is limited to include only those units that involve over 75 total students. Finally, the map is sorted (in descending order) by the total number periods involved.

The last map represents just the social studies curriculum, K-12. This map would be valuable for planning integrated Big Six Skills and social studies instruction. It would also be useful to the social studies department in their overall curriculum planning efforts.

---

* This is only one possible approach to determining priorities. In other situations, the library media specialist may wish to key on units with other characteristics, e.g., organized in small groups and in subject areas not typically involved with library & information skills instruction.

Curriculum Map 2: K-12 Example

Only Those Records Where Resources Are Not Just Text and Evaluation Is Not Just a Test

Sorted by
GRADE   54   Units

Gr	Course	Unit	Mk P	Per	#Std	#Sn	Level	Method	Resources	Org	Evaluation
01-01	Math	Whole/Parts	0011	20	22	1	I	lect/desk	wkbk	L/I	wksheet
02-02	Science	Birds	0010	13	120	4	I	combin 4	multiple	L/S	product/obs
02-02	Science	Measurement	0100	15	28	1	I	combin 5	worksheet	S/I	test/obs
02-02	Science	Weather	0100	10	28	1	I/R	combin 6	text/packet	L/I	test/report
03-03	English	Biographies	0010	15	26	1	R/E	combin 3	multiple	L	report
03-03	SS	Important Persons	0001	15	34	1	I	report	multiple	I	report
04-04	English	Poetry	0100	25	27	1	I/R/E	lect/discuss	multiple	L/S	product/obs
04-04	English	Public Speaking	0011	15	27	1	I/R	demo/practi	multiple	L	speech
04-04	Math	Graphing	0001	10	34	1	R/E	lect/desk	text/worksheet	L/I	test/product
04-04	Science	Dinosaurs	0010	10	28	1	I	combin 3	multiple	L/S/I	product
04-04	Science	Weather	0110	50	28	1	I/R	combin 6	text/packet	L/I	test/report
04-04	Science	Weather/Climate	0010	10	27	1	I/R	combin 5	multiple	S/I	combin 3
04-04	SS	Careers	0001	25	29	1	I	combin 6	multiple	L/S/I	product
04-04	SS	Erie Canal	0100	15	120	4	I/R/E	combin 5	multiple	L/S/I	product
05-05	Science	Astronomy	0010	15	26	1	I	combin 5	multiple	S	product
05-05	SS	Exploration	1000	15	29	1	I	combin 5	text/multiple	L/S	product
05-06	SS	Map-It	0100	25	120	4	R/E	combin 4	multiple	L/I	product
06-06	Science	Energy	0001	30	27	1	I/R	demo/discu	multiple	L	test/product
07-07	English 7	Research Project	0010	15	122	4	I/R/E	combin 3	multiple	L/S/I	report
07-07	English 7	Travel Brochures	0110	9	120	4	R/E	combin 5	multiple	L/I	product
07-07	Health	Nutrition	1010	20	180	8	R/E	combin 4	multiple	L/S/I	test/product
07-07	Home/Careers	Nutrition	1000	10	98	5	I/R/E	combin 7	text/multiple	L/S/I	combin 4
07-07	Music	Composers	0100	10	150	3	I/R	combin 4	multiple	L/I	report
07-07	Science 7	Plants	0001	25	125	4	R/E	combin 7	multiple	S/I	test/product
07-07	SS 7	Colonialization	0100	25	112	5	I/E	combin 4	text/multiple	I	test/obs
07-07	SS 7	Current Events	1111	40	75	3	I/E	discuss	multiple	L	test/product
07-09	Math/Special	Decimals	0110	20	12	1	R/E	combin 3	text/multiple	L/I	test/wksheet
07-09	PE	Dance - Rythms	0010	8	185	5	I/R/E	demo/practi	none	L	test/obs
07-09	PE	Softball	0001	8	720	5	R/E	lect/demo	multiple	L	obs

Gr = Grade I Mk P = Marking Period I Per = Periods I #Std = Number of Students I #Sn = Number of Sections I Org= Organization of Instruction
For Level, I = Introduce, R = Reinforce, E = Expand. For Organization, L = Large Group, S = Small Group, I = Individual

Gr	Course	Unit	Mk P	Per	#Std	#Sn	Level	Method	Resources	Org	Evaluation
08-08	English 8	Diary of Anne	0110	20	66	3	I/R/E	combin 5	one/multi	L/S/I	combin 3
08-08	Reading	Words	0010	15	120	4	I/R/E	combin 4	multiple	L/I	present
08-08	Science 8	Energy	0010	60	99	3	I/R/E	combin 5	text/multiple	L/S	test/product
09-09	English 9	Poetry	0100	15	112	4	I/R/E	combin 4	text/multiple	L/I	written
09-09	English 9	Shakespeare	0001	30	112	4	I	combin 6	text/multiple	L/I	combin 3
09-09	English 9	Thematic	0010	9	120	4	R/E	combin 5	multiple	L/I	present
09-09	English 9	Vocabulary	1111	40	112	4	R/E	desk work	dictionary	L/I	wksheet
09-09	Home/Careers	Food and Nutrition	0011	30	135	5	I/R/E	combin 6	text/multiple	L/S/I	combin 4
09-09	Science/Earth	Weather	0010	15	98	4	I/R/E	combin 4	text/multiple	L/S/I	test/product
09-09	SS 9	Africa	0100	30	28	2	I	combin 4	multiple	L	test/report
09-09	SS 9	China	0010	30	94	5	I/R/E	combin 8	text/multiple	L/S/I	test/product
09-10	Spanish 2	Christmas Customs	0100	5	55	2	I/R	lect/discuss	text/multiple	L	test/product
09-10	Spanish 2	Geography	0010	10	55	2	R/E	combin 4	text/multiple	L/S/I	combin 3
09-12	Music	Band Rehearsal	1111	180	80	1	I/R/E	demo	one source	L	obs
10-10	Guidance	Career Planning	0001	5	360	12	R/E	project	multiple	I	product
10-10	SS 10/English	Global Problems	0100	11	120	4	R/E	combin 3	multiple	L/I	project
10-12	Health	Disease	0101	20	250	10	I/R/E	combin 4	text/multiple	L	test/product
10-12	Health	Tobacco/Smoking	1010	20	250	10	R/E	combin 5	multiple	L/I	combin 3
10-12	Spanish 3	Que Pasa?	0001	9	50	2	E	combin 3	multiple	S	product
11-11	English 11	Mystery/Suspense	0001	30	115	5	I/R/E	combin 5	multiple	S/I	project
11-11	SS 11	Biography/Women	1000	10	115	5	I	discuss/proj	multiple	S/I	report
11-11	SS 11	Civil War	0010	20	110	4	R/E	combin 5	text/multiple	L/S/I	combin 4
11-11	SS 11	Timeline - U.S.	0100	3	80	4	R/E	lect/desk	multiple	L/I	wksheet
11-12	SS/Sociology	The Family	0001	12	30	1	E	combin 4	multiple	L/I	product
12-12	SS/Economics	Corporate Profiles	0010	20	23	1	E	combin 3	multiple	L/I	product

.

Gr = Grade I Mk P = Marking Period I Per = Periods I #Std = Number of Students I #Sn = Number of Sections I Org= Organization of Instruction
For Level, I = Introduce, R = Reinforce, E = Expand. For Organization, L = Large Group, S = Small Group, I = Individual

Curriculum Map 2: K-12 Example

Only Those Records Where Resources Are Not Just Text and Evaluation Is Not Just a Test

Sorted by
MARKING PERIOD   54   Units

Mk P	Gr	Course	Unit	Per	#Std	#Sn	Level	Method	Resources	Org	Evaluation
1111	07-07	SS 7	Current Events	40	75	3	I/E	discuss	multiple	L	test/product
1111	09-09	English 9	Vocabulary	40	112	4	R/E	desk work	dictionary	L/I	wksheet
1111	09-12	Music	Band Rehearsal	180	80	1	I/R/E	demo	one source	L	obs
1010	07-07	Health	Nutrition	20	180	8	R/E	combin 4	multiple	L/S/I	test/product
1010	10-12	Health	Tobacco/Smoking	20	250	10	R/E	combin 5	multiple	L/I	combin 3
1000	05-05	SS	Exploration	15	29	1	I	combin 5	text/multiple	L/S	product
1000	07-07	Home/Careers	Nutrition	10	98	5	I/R/E	combin 7	text/multiple	L/S/I	combin 4
1000	11-11	SS 11	Biography/Women	10	115	5	I	discuss/proj	multiple	S/I	report
0110	04-04	Science	Weather	50	28	1	I/R	combin 6	text/packet	L/I	test/report
0110	07-07	English 7	Travel Brochures	9	120	4	R/E	combin 5	multiple	L/I	product
0110	07-09	Math/Special	Decimals	20	12	1	R/E	combin 3	text/multiple	L/I	test/wksheet
0110	08-08	English 8	Diary of Anne	20	66	3	I/R/E	combin 5	one/multi	L/S/I	combin 3
0101	10-12	Health	Disease	20	250	10	I/R/E	combin 4	text/multiple	L	test/product
0100	02-02	Science	Weather	10	28	1	I/R	combin 6	text/packet	L/I	test/report
0100	02-02	Science	Measurement	15	28	1	I	combin 5	worksheet	S/I	test/obs
0100	04-04	SS	Erie Canal	15	120	4	I/R/E	combin 5	multiple	L/S/I	product
0100	04-04	English	Poetry	25	27	1	I/R/E	lect/discuss	multiple	L/S	product/obs
0100	05-06	SS	Map-It	25	120	4	R/E	combin 4	multiple	L/I	product
0100	07-07	SS 7	Colonialization	25	112	5	I/E	combin 4	text/multiple	I	test/obs
0100	07-07	Music	Composers	10	150	3	I/R	combin 4	multiple	L/I	report
0100	09-09	English 9	Poetry	15	112	4	I/R/E	combin 4	text/multiple	L/I	written
0100	09-09	SS 9	Africa	30	28	2	I	combin 4	multiple	L	test/report
0100	09-10	Spanish 2	Christmas Customs	5	55	2	I/R	lect/discuss	text/multiple	L	test/product
0100	10-10	SS 10/English	Global Problems	11	120	4	R/E	combin 3	multiple	L/I	project
0100	11-11	SS 11	Timeline - U.S.	3	80	4	R/E	lect/desk	multiple	L/I	wksheet
0011	01-01	Math	Whole/Parts	20	22	1	I	lect/desk	wkbk	L/I	wksheet
0011	04-04	English	Public Speaking	15	27	1	I/R	demo/practi	multiple	L	speech
0011	09-09	Home/Careers	Food and Nutrition	30	135	5	I/R/E	combin 6	text/multiple	L/S/I	combin 4

Gr = Grade I Mk P = Marking Period I Per = Periods I #Std = Number of Students I #Sn = Number of Sections I Org= Organization of Instruction
For Level, I = Introduce, R = Reinforce, E = Expand. For Organization, L = Large Group, S = Small Group, I = Individual

Mk P Gr		Course	Unit	Per	#Std	#Sn	Level	Method	Resources	Org	Evaluation
0010	02-02	Science	Birds	13	120	4	I	combin 4	multiple	L/S	product/obs
0010	03-03	English	Biographies	15	26	1	R/E	combin 3	multiple	L	report
0010	04-04	Science	Dinosaurs	10	28	1	I	combin 3	multiple	L/S/I	product
0010	04-04	Science	Weather/Climate	10	27	1	I/R	combin 5	multiple	S/I	combin 3
0010	05-05	Science	Astronomy	15	26	1	I	combin 5	multiple	S	product
0010	07-07	English 7	Research Project	15	122	4	I/R/E	combin 3	multiple	L/S/I	report
0010	07-09	PE	Dance - Rythms	8	185	5	I/R/E	demo/practi	none	L	test/obs
0010	08-08	Science 8	Energy	60	99	3	I/R/E	combin 5	text/multiple	L/S	test/product
0010	08-08	Reading	Words	15	120	4	I/R/E	combin 4	multiple	L/I	present
0010	09-09	English 9	Thematic	9	120	4	R/E	combin 5	multiple	L/I	present
0010	09-09	SS 9	China	30	94	5	I/R/E	combin 8	text/multiple	L/S/I	test/product
0010	09-09	Science/Earth	Weather	15	98	4	I/R/E	combin 4	text/multiple	L/S/I	test/product
0010	09-10	Spanish 2	Geography	10	55	2	R/E	combin 4	text/multiple	L/S/I	combin 3
0010	11-11	SS 11	Civil War	20	110	4	R/E	combin 5	text/multiple	L/S/I	combin 4
0010	12-12	SS/Economics	Corporate Profiles	20	23	1	E	combin 3	multiple	L/I	product
0001	03-03	SS	Important Persons	15	34	1	I	report	multiple	I	report
0001	04-04	Math	Graphing	10	34	1	R/E	lect/desk	text/worksheet	L/I	test/product
0001	04-04	SS	Careers	25	29	1	I	combin 6	multiple	L/S/I	product
0001	06-06	Science	Energy	30	27	1	I/R	demo/discu	multiple	L	test/product
0001	07-07	Science 7	Plants	25	125	4	R/E	combin 7	multiple	S/I	test/product
0001	07-09	PE	Softball	8	720	5	R/E	lect/demo	multiple	L	obs
0001	09-09	English 9	Shakespeare	30	112	4	I	combin 6	text/multiple	L/I	combin 3
0001	10-10	Guidance	Career Planning	5	360	12	R/E	project	multiple	I	product
0001	10-12	Spanish 3	Que Pasa?	9	50	2	E	combin 3	multiple	S	product
0001	11-11	English 11	Mystery/Suspense	30	115	5	I/R/E	combin 5	multiple	S/I	project
0001	11-12	SS/Sociology	The Family	12	30	1	E	combin 4	multiple	L/I	product

Gr = Grade | Mk P = Marking Period | Per = Periods | #Std = Number of Students | #Sn = Number of Sections | Org= Organization of Instruction
For Level, I = Introduce, R = Reinforce, E = Expand. For Organization, L = Large Group, S = Small Group, I = Individual

Curriculum Map 3: K-12 Example

Only Those Records Where: Resources Are Multiple, Evaluation Is A Report or a Product, and
the Number of Students is 75 or Greater

Sorted (descending)
by PERIODS
          15   Units

Per	Gr	Course	Unit	Mk P	#Std	#Sn	Level	Method	Resources	Org	Evaluation
60	08-08	Science 8	Energy	0010	99	3	I/R/E	combin 5	text/multiple	L/S	test/product
40	07-07	SS 7	Current Events	1111	75	3	I/E	discuss	multiple	L	test/product
30	09-09	SS 9	China	0010	94	5	I/R/E	combin 8	text/multiple	L/S/I	test/product
25	05-06	SS	Map-It	0100	120	4	R/E	combin 4	multiple	L/I	product
25	07-07	Science 7	Plants	0001	125	4	R/E	combin 7	multiple	S/I	test/product
20	07-07	Health	Nutrition	1010	180	8	R/E	combin 4	multiple	L/S/I	test/product
20	10-12	Health	Disease	0101	250	10	I/R/E	combin 4	text/multiple	L	test/product
15	04-04	SS	Erie Canal	0100	120	4	I/R/E	combin 5	multiple	L/S/I	product
15	07-07	English 7	Research Project	0010	122	4	I/R/E	combin 3	multiple	L/S/I	report
15	09-09	Science/Earth	Weather	0010	98	4	I/R/E	combin 4	text/multiple	L/S/I	test/product
13	02-02	Science	Birds	0010	120	4	I	combin 4	multiple	L/S	product/obs
10	07-07	Music	Composers	0100	150	3	I/R	combin 4	multiple	L/I	report
10	11-11	SS 11	Biography/Women	1000	115	5	I	discuss/proj	multiple	S/I	report
9	07-07	English 7	Travel Brochures	0110	120	4	R/E	combin 5	multiple	L/I	product
5	10-10	Guidance	Career Planning	0001	360	12	R/E	project	multiple	I	product

Gr = Grade I Mk P = Marking Period I Per = Periods I #Std = Number of Students I #Sn = Number of Sections I Org= Organization of Instruction
For Level, I = Introduce, R = Reinforce, E = Expand. For Organization, L = Large Group, S = Small Group, I = Individual

Curriculum Map 4: K-12 Example
SOCIAL STUDIES CURRICULUM

Sorted by GRADE   19   Units

Gr	Course	Unit	Mk P	Per	#Std	#Sn	Level	Method	Resources	Org	Evaluation
03-03	SS	Important Persons	0001	15	34	1	I	report	multiple	I	report
04-04	SS	Careers	0001	25	29	1	I	combin 6	multiple	L/S/I	product
04-04	SS	Erie Canal	0100	15	120	4	I/R/E	combin 5	multiple	L/S/I	product
05-05	SS	Exploration	1000	15	29	1	I	combin 5	text/multiple	L/S	product
05-06	SS	Map-It	0100	25	120	4	R/E	combin 4	multiple	L/I	product
07-07	SS 7	Colonialization	0100	25	112	5	I/E	combin 4	text/multiple	I	test/obs
07-07	SS 7	Current Events	1111	40	75	3	I/E	discuss	multiple	L	test/product
07-07	SS 7	Exploration	1000	15	77	4	I/E	combin 3	text/multiple	L	test
08-08	SS 8	American Symbols	1000	15	108	4	R/E	combin 4	multiple	L	test
08-08	SS 8	Civil War	0010	20	88	3	I/R	lect/disc	text	L	test
08-08	SS 8	Constitution	1000	20	78	3	R	lect/desk	text	L/I	test
09-09	SS 9	Africa	0100	30	28	2	I	combin 4	multiple	L	test/report
09-09	SS 9	China	0010	30	94	5	I/R/E	combin 8	text/multiple	L/S/I	test/product
10-10	SS 10/English	Global Problems	0100	11	120	4	R/E	combin 3	multiple	L/I	project
11-11	SS 11	Biography/Women	1000	10	115	5	I	discuss/proj	multiple	S/I	report
11-11	SS 11	Civil War	0010	20	110	4	R/E	combin 5	text/multiple	L/S/I	combin 4
11-11	SS 11	Timeline - U.S.	0100	3	80	4	R/E	lect/desk	multiple	L/I	wksheet
11-12	SS/Sociology	The Family	0001	12	30	1	E	combin 4	multiple	L/I	product
12-12	SS/Economics	Corporate Profiles	0010	20	23	1	E	combin 3	multiple	L/I	product

Gr = Grade I Mk P = Marking Period I Per = Periods I #Std = Number of Students I #Sn = Number of Sections I Org= Organization of Instruction
For Level, I = Introduce, R = Reinforce, E = Expand. For Organization, L = Large Group, S = Small Group, I = Individual

Bibliography

American Association of School Librarians and Association for Educational Communications and Technology. *Information Power: Guidelines for School Library Media Programs*. Chicago, IL: American Library Association, 1988.

Craver, Kathleen W. "The Changing Instructional Role of the High School Library Media Specialist: 1950-84." *School Library Media Quarterly* 14, no. 4 (Summer, 1986): 183-191.

Cutlip, Glen W. *Learning and Information: Skills for the Secondary Classroom and Library Media Program*. Englewood, CO: Libraries Unlimited, 1988.

Eisenberg, Michael B. "Curriculum Mapping and Implementation of an Elementary School Library Media Skills Curriculum." *School Library Media Quarterly* 12, no. 2 (Fall 1984): 411-418.

Eisenberg, Michael B. and Berkowitz, Robert E. *Curriculum Initiative: An Agenda and Strategy for Library Media Programs*. Norwood, NJ: Ablex, 1988.

Eisenberg, Michael B. and Berkowitz, Robert E. *Resource Companion to Curriculum Initiative: An Agenda and Strategy for Library Media Programs*. Norwood, NJ: Ablex, 1988.

English, Fenwick W. *Quality Control in Curriculum Development*. Alexandria, VA: American Association of School Administrators, 1978.

Ewing, David. "Discover Your Problem-Solving Style." *Psychology Today* 11, no.7 (December 1977): p. 69-70, 73, 138.

Irving, Ann. *Study and Information Skills Across the Curriculum*. London: Heinemann Educational Books, 1985.

Koberg, Don, and Bagnall, Jim. *The Universal Traveler, A Soft-Systems Guide to Creativity, Problem-Solving and the Process of Reaching Goals*. Los Altos, CA: William Kaufmann, 1980.

Krimmelbein, Cindy Jeffrey. *The Choice to Change: Establishing an Integrated School Library Media Program*. Littleton, CO: Libraries Unlimited, 1989.

Kuhlthau, Carol Collier. "Information Search Process: A Summary of Research and Implications for School Library Media Programs." *School Library Media Quarterly* 18, no. 1 (Fall 1989): 19-25.

Kuhlthau, Carol Collier. "An Emerging Theory of Library Instruction." *School Library Media Quarterly* 16, no. 1 (Fall 1987): 23-28.

Kuhlthau, Carol Collier. "A Process Approach to Library Skills Instruction." *School Library Media Quarterly* 13, no. 2 (Winter 1985): 35-40.

Kuhlthau, Carol Collier. *Teaching the Library Research Process.* West Nyack, NY: The Center for Applied Research in Education, 1985.

Large, Peter. *The Micro Revolution Revisited.* Totowa, NJ: Rowman and Allenheld Co., 1984.

Liesener, James W. *Learning at Risk: School Library Media Programs in an Information World.* Office of Educational Research and Improvement, Center for Libraries and Education Improvement, Washington, DC, 1984. (ED 243 889). In *School Library Media Quarterly* 13, no. 1 (Fall 1985).

Library Media Skills into Content Areas. Harrisburg, PA: Bureau of State Library, Division of School Library Media Services, Pennsylvania Department of Education, 1988.

Loertscher, David. *Taxonomies of the School Library Media Program.* Englewood, CO: Libraries Unlimited, 1988.

Mancall, Jacqueline C., Aaron, Shirley L., and Walker, Sue A. "Educating Students to Think: The Role of the School Library Media Program." *School Library Media Quarterly* 14, no. 3 (Fall 1986): 18-47.

Markuson, Carolyn. "Making It Happen: Taking Charge of the Information Curriculum." *School Library Media Quarterly* 15, no. 1 (Fall 1986): 37-40. (EJ 344 242).

Matrix for Curriculum Planning in Library Media and Information Skills Education. Madison, WI: Wisconsin Department of Public Instruction, 1989.

Naisbitt, John. *Megatrends: Ten New Directions Transforming Our Lives.* New York, NY: Warner Books, 1982.

Stripling, Barbara K. and Judy M. Pitts. *Brainstorms and Blueprints: Teaching Library Research as a Thinking Process.* Englewood, CO: Libraries Unlimited, 1988.

Turner, Philip. *Helping Teachers Teach.* Littleton, CO: Libraries Unlimited, 1985.

Turner, Philip (Ed.). *A Casebook for "Helping Teachers Teach."* Englewood, CO: Libraries Unlimited, 1988

Walker, H. Thomas and Montgomery, Paula Kay. *Teaching Library Media Skills.* 2nd ed.. Littleton, CO: Libraries Unlimited, 1983.

Index